T0399641

THE ART OF KNIFE FIGHTING FOR STAGE AND SCREEN

The Art of Knife Fighting for Stage and Screen: An Actor's and Director's Guide to Staged Violence provides detailed information for the safe use of knives and daggers in a theatrical setting and an in-depth understanding of safe theatrical weapons.

The book starts with an extensive safety review, then moves on to the basic techniques of dagger fighting, starting with grip and body postures. Readers will then learn about the basic actions of cuts, parries, blocks, and disarms. During this process, they will explore the connection between body and weapon and start learning the elements of storytelling through choreography. Special attention is given to suicides, threats, and murder and how directors, choreographers, performers, teachers, and students can approach these techniques in a way that is physically and mentally safe. The book also covers the use of throwing knives, knife flips, and other tricks to help add a little flair to your fight.

The Art of Knife Fighting for Stage and Screen teaches the safe theatrical use of the knife for directors, performers, educators, and students of stage combat.

Erick Vaughn Wolfe is the current Chair of Theatre, Co-Director of Musical Theatre, and Program Director for the Arts Management and Leadership program at Missouri Southern State University in Joplin, Missouri. He earned his BFA in Performance from Oklahoma Central University and his MFA in Film and Theatre Directing from the University of New Orleans. He is a certified teacher with both the British Academy of Dramatic Combat (BADC) and Academy of Performance Combat (APC). Erick has been working in film, theatre, opera, ballet, and musical theatre for over 20 years as a fight choreographer, stunt performer, and director. After running his own stage combat training center for 10 years, Erick traveled around teaching combat and movement across the United States and the United Kingdom before entering teaching at the university level.

THE ART OF KNIFE FIGHTING FOR STAGE AND SCREEN

An Actor's and Director's Guide to Staged Violence

Erick Vaughn Wolfe

Routledge
Taylor & Francis Group

NEW YORK AND LONDON

Cover image: Heday Inoue and Lucia Lucas in Tulsa Opera's production of Don Giovanni, Directed by Denni Sayers. Photo courtesy of Shane Bevel.

First published 2022
by Routledge
605 Third Avenue, New York, NY 10158

and by Routledge
2 Park Square, Milton Park, Abingdon, Oxon, OX14 4RN

Routledge is an imprint of the Taylor & Francis Group, an informa business

© 2022 Erick Vaughn Wolfe

Library of Congress Cataloging-in-Publication Data
Names: Wolfe, Erick Vaughn, author.
Title: The art of knife fighting for stage and screen : an actor's and director's guide to staged violence / Erick Vaughn Wolfe.
Description: New York, NY : Routledge, 2022. | Includes index.
Identifiers: LCCN 2021037724 (print) | LCCN 2021037725 (ebook) | ISBN 9780367707613 (hardback) | ISBN 9780367707606 (paperback) | ISBN 9781003147862 (ebook)
Subjects: LCSH: Stage combat. | Knife fighting.
Classification: LCC PN2071.F5 W65 2022 (print) | LCC PN2071.F5 (ebook) | DDC 792.02/8—dc23
LC record available at https://lccn.loc.gov/2021037724
LC ebook record available at https://lccn.loc.gov/2021037725

ISBN: 978-0-367-70761-3 (hbk)
ISBN: 978-0-367-70760-6 (pbk)
ISBN: 978-1-003-14786-2 (ebk)

DOI: 10.4324/9781003147862

Typeset in Joanna
by Apex CoVantage, LLC

To Viviane

To my parents

To Teachers and Friends who, with passion and dedication, teach these arts safely.

To the Students who carry our legacies forward and blaze new paths in the performance world.

"Now we take up the dagger. God preserve us all!"

— Hans Talhoffer, 1467

CONTENTS

FOREWORD
Lloyd N. Caldwell

Erick and I met when I was first appointed to Oklahoma State University (OSU). We were both fight directors, so it was natural that we traveled in the same orbit. I would drop into his school in Tulsa on occasion, and we'd compare notes on the business of running a commercial stage combat school, which I had done in my pre-academic life. He later joined my professional organization, the British Academy of Dramatic Combat, as a certified instructor, and we had the opportunity to teach together in Wales.

A few years into my time at OSU, a friend from England, Rachel Bown-Williams, got in touch with me to see if she could come and study for a few days. I was pleased to offer our home to her, and I reached out to Erick to form a "third", providing Rachel a partner to work with as we explored several styles.

I had taught what was then euphemistically called "combatives" for the army during my time as a company grade officer, and later had the privilege of supervising combative training in a service school for elite infantry. These courses concentrated on unarmed and knife combat. As a fight director, I had begun to adapt these lessons to the realm of stage combat.

On the weekend Rachel arrived, the three of us decided to concentrate on knife work. Erick was quite taken with the knife. In skilled hands the knife is deadly, of course. But there is also an entire aesthetic to some schools of knife fighting which are quite dramatic and beautiful. The Filipino styles, in particular, are intricate and engrossing. The difficulty in adapting knife work to stage combat lies in speed. As is true of sword and fisticuffs, an actual knife fight is over in fractions of a second. This is too soon for an audience to integrate the action into the overall narrative of the play or film.

We explored rhythm and phrasing and integration of different knife styles into each other for better "storytelling". I taught them the difference between combat knife technique and the more exotic forms. We choreographed several stage combat phrases and adjusted them to different partner pairings.

We had a terrific time in the backyard until Erick brought out his bullwhips. In learning to crack whips, we created the soundscape of a small-arms firefight that my new neighbors took exception to, and so the day drew to a premature close.

If you are reading this book, you really do not need me to define stage combat or fight directing – unlike my poor neighbors, who had no clue who'd just moved in! I will dispense with that discussion to move on to why this book is so important.

While we are storytellers, we tell not the entire story but a very specific portion of it. Stage violence is usually the culmination of dramatic events. It either puts an end to a conflict between characters or leads directly to that conclusion. It should be exciting, as stage violence often occurs at the penultimate moment of tension. In order to bring the audience along, we must adjust whatever combat technique we use so that it is observable, identifiable, and immediate.

I love fencing. I have been a fencer since the age of 16. I fenced in college and in the army and I am, alas, in a decided minority. We no longer study the art of the sword outside of stage combat, stunt, and sporting circles. If you have observed someone routinely carrying a sword in your community, I suggest you move out!

Swords are an anachronism. We as a society have abandoned these weapons. We rely on courts and the police. While domestic violence is very regrettably still with us, other forms of armed personal combat are rare. When they do take place, they usually involve guns or knives.

We have all heard about someone being attacked with a knife. Through television news, it is part of our life experience. It is relatable.

It is also immediate. We all have that knife in the kitchen that we are instinctively careful in handling. It's big, it's sharp, and it is, in a way, elementally scary. We recognize its utility in preparing food and its potentiality in causing harm.

The knife is contemporary. In the theatre, we mount plays from centuries ago. The plays of William Shakespeare are perennial favorites, though increasingly we see plays by John Ford, Richard Sheridan, John Webster, and the like. These plays contain scenes of personal combat employing knife and dagger. In order to make these plays accessible to modern audiences, directors place them in modern garb and modern settings. The concept holds water until swords are introduced. As a consequence, there has been for some time a movement toward substituting knives for swords.

As a purely practical matter, an armory of swords is quite expensive to own and maintain and quite beyond the reach of most theatre companies. Blunted knives, or specifically fabricated knives in aluminum, are much more affordable.

What remains of the theatrical equation set forth earlier – observable, identifiable, immediate – is the observable. This is where the book you currently hold comes in. It is in the technique that the theatrical potential of knife work is realized. How does one perform a creditable duel with knives safely and with enough craft that the storytelling is clear, concise, and riveting? Erick will lay out the method in the following chapters.

I am immensely gratified that Erick pursued this line of scholarship. He has certainly surpassed my knowledge and skill. Most of the stage combat organizations in the world offering training now have curricula specifically focused on the knife. There are few books which contain a chapter on stage combat knife.

This monograph is the first to offer an in-depth discussion of the topic, and I am thrilled to recommend it to you.

Lloyd N. Caldwell
Fight Director
Stillwater, Oklahoma

ACKNOWLEDGEMENTS

This book would not have been possible without the support from so many individuals and organizations throughout my career – starting with being introduced to professional stage combat by a great mentor and Olympic fencing coach, Jerry Benson, back in the mid-1990s. Through his guidance and instruction, a kid who loved to play with swords at Renaissance festivals started on a path that would take him all over the world and would eventually go from a hobby to a career. Years later, after moving and starting on this new path, Dr. Lloyd Caldwell called me up one fateful day. Without his guidance, patience, mentorship, and – even more valuable – friendship, I would never have transitioned into a full-time fight director, nor would I have ever considered teaching at the academic level. These two men challenged me and changed my life for the better, and I owe each of them more than could ever be expressed in words. What I can do is take their lessons and pass them on to my students.

My professional training with the British Academy of Dramatic Combat was world changing. Working with great instructors such as Kev McCurdy, Ian McCracken, Andrew Ashenden, Rachel Bown-Williams, John Greenwood, and many others, I learned not only techniques but also the teaching and philosophy of our art form. I carry these individuals with me in every class or workshop I teach. To all the teachers and colleagues I have had the fortune to study, work, train, or just share a space with, thank you so much!

In the opera world, there are two individuals whose friendship, mentorship, and encouragement have made my life all the better. Kostis Protopapas and Rachel Ginzberg have been a part of my life for almost 20 years, and I hope they will be for many more. If not for the two of them, my career in opera would not be what it is today, and for that there are not enough words of gratitude.

This book would not be what it is if it were not for the technical editing of Kevin Inouye. Kevin and I have known each other for over a decade, and it is a friendship I value dearly. Watching his career grow fills my heart with joy.

On a personal level, there are individuals whose love and friendship gave me the fortitude to keep on this path. My two brothers, Dr. Blake Dills and Dr. David Sharlow, were always there with encouragement, beer, and a kick in the butt when needed.

To Viviane, without whom none of this, both literally and figuratively, would be possible.

To my remarkable parents, who introduced their only child to the world of the arts at a young age and encouraged me to never give up.

Finally, to all my students past and present. Teaching you is one of my life's greatest joys. I have learned so much from all of you – thank you.

1

INTRODUCTION

Why the knife? What is it about this weapon?

I have always loved knife fighting. The intimacy of the close action and the immediacy of the fight are elements that have drawn this weapon to the forefront for writers for centuries. You will find knives and daggers in historical plays all the way up to modern theatre, opera, ballet, television, film, video games, and musicals. When directors want to update a production, instead of using swords, they often opt for the knife.

This book is designed to cover an area in stage combat that is currently lacking attention, though I find that it is one of the most highly used and common weapons on stage and set: the knife. If you are a student of theatre, a beginning or seasoned actor, a director, a fight choreographer, a teacher, or just an enthusiast, this book is for you. I will cover a wide range of information. Some of this information you may know and some may be new, but all of it will be relevant to understanding how to utilize the weapon in training or performance.

DOI: 10.4324/9781003147862-1

The focus of the material in this book is on safety. If you have never used a knife on stage before, just need brushing up on your technique, are looking to improve your skills, or want to expand your experience, this book can help. One of the most important things to remember about this book is understanding that it is intended for education in theatrical combat. It does not aim to teach you how to fight someone with a real knife. All actions in this book are designed to be performed with the proper theatrical equipment, under the guidance of a professional certified stage combat instructor or choreographer.

The layout of this book is intended to flow like a workshop, each section building on the previous methods and techniques discussed – starting with a conversation about safety and understanding of theatrical combat. This is followed by grips and stances, as these two elements immediately tell the story of the characters holding the weapons. Aggressive, passive, scared, trained, or untrained all become instantly understandable to the audience the moment a character grabs their weapon and gets into a position to fight. It is these details that make a fight dynamic and exciting to watch.

The next few chapters deal with the technical elements of knife and dagger fighting. The elements explored extend to essential and advanced footwork. Footwork is literally and figuratively the foundation of all good fights. Body dynamics, such as bobbing, weaving, and leaning, can break up a static moment. But do not get me wrong; sometimes stillness sets the tension needed.

Exploring the actions of attacks, blocks, and defenses build your skills as you learn the elements and variations that will set the stage for the choreography. The multiple ways in which these base actions can be combined is the inner core of your action scenes. These techniques must be mastered to be precise and controlled. Of the written choreography, this is 90% of the action. This is your technical element to the fight.

Once the technical elements are mastered, we then get introduced to advanced actions of grabs, checks, and disarms. Now we are putting the personality into the choreography. How skilled are the characters, and what is the level of danger in the fight for them? Here we start talking about how the character must be in danger but the actor must be safe, and we also talk about victim control. We expand the advanced actions with the next section on threats, cuts, murders, and suicide.

I would like to pause here a moment and talk to you about actor safety. In this book, I don't just address an actor's physical safety but also address the performers' mental safety. When dealing with issues such as being threatened with a weapon, self-harm, or the subjects of suicide and rape, we must be actively aware of our performers' mental health safety. Always address these issues long before you start choreographing a moment. I talk about this later in the book; however, I want you to start thinking about these issues as soon as possible.

We spend a chapter working on the techniques of threats, cuts, murders, and suicide. These subjects should not be approached lightly, and safety is of the utmost focus for a successful choreography. One focus of this is the line of sight with the audience and how staging will help tell the story and keep the actors safe. Then we add some flair to our fights, where we explore the use of offhand protection, towels, double knives, knife grip flips, and how to throw a knife on stage.

The chapters close out with final thoughts for actors and directors. Here, all the ideas we covered in the previous chapters are brought together to look at what makes a good, safe fight and how to create that dynamic, high-energy choreography in the space and time you have. The glossary is filled with terms and concepts, and the book concludes with appendices that list out various resources that I hope you find useful.

I hope you enjoy this book. It was a passion project of mine, and to be honest, if there is a good response to it, I will happily produce a second volume that goes into so much more detail on different fighting styles and different types of knives and daggers and their use. But this book is a beginning, a starting place for those who are excited to start stepping into the world of knife chorography. So if you enjoy it, or find some of it useful or interesting, drop me a line. Let us talk and get to know each other.

I welcome you, and I hope you have a wonderful, exciting, and safe journey.

2

THE ELEMENTS OF THEATRICAL VIOLENCE

Safety: First and Foremost

It has been so many years now that I do not remember who I first heard it from, but one of my first lessons in safety was the simple phrase: "The more out of control the character is, the more in control the actor has to be". I have kept that in the forefront of all my work and pass it to every actor and student I work with.

If you read this book chapter by chapter, you will get a sense of repetition about one principle of stage combat that I feel is the most important aspect – safety. Safety is at the heart of everything we do when we teach, choreograph, or perform any type of violence for stage or screen. A safe choreography is also a repeatable choreography. We should never allow an actor to be in danger physically or emotionally. We should never allow anyone – including the cast, crew, or audience – to be in any form of danger. I take this to heart, and it has been my guiding principle my

DOI: 10.4324/978-003147862-2

entire career. Acted aggression is a dangerous business on its own. Actors can get caught up in the moment, adrenaline can spike, or countless other things can go wrong. Add to these moments a weapon – especially a weapon like a knife or dagger, something small that requires the performers to get close to each other – and the possibility for accidents or injuries doubles. Therefore, we must always keep safety first and foremost in all our work.

But there is a dark side to this. A fight must not look excessively safe to the audience. If the audience does not feel a sense of connection to the characters and does not feel engaged or invested in the dangers of the fight for the characters, then we are defeating our second rule: Serve the story. Notice that I said *characters* and not *actors*. Keep the actors safe, but put the characters in danger. A fight, or a moment of choreography, must be a part of the total story being told. It must fit in seamlessly with the previous actions and flow into the next segment of the show. We must continue the audience's willing suspension of disbelief. Fights are used for many reasons in a story, such as setting conflicts (think the opening fight of *Romeo and Juliet*), sending a protagonist on their journey (think *Star Wars: A New Hope*), or the final resolution of building conflict, which includes too many to name here. Whatever the reason for the inclusion of the fight, it must fit within the world the director has created. All too often I have witnessed a fight, usually choreographed by someone just starting out, that just sticks out from the rest of the show. It is either too slow, too far apart, the actors break character and are just mindlessly performing chorography with no acting behind it, or the choreographer wants to put in all the cool and flashy moves they can think of for that "wow" factor. First, good job on keeping everyone safe; you followed the first rule. However, there is no story or continuity to the action. Therefore, you failed the second rule. Yet to be honest, this is the hardest part of fight direction to learn. When I was first starting out, I was guilty of all those actions at one time or another, but fortunately I had people around who helped and mentored my growth as a choreographer and director. The technical elements, the actual stage combat, take work and practice under the guidance of a qualified teacher. Learning how to be a fight director or choreographer takes time and understanding. You need to fully understand story structure, lines of sight, vocalization, intent, collaboration with all the designers and directors, and performers' physical and emotional boundaries, and never forget a little bit of stage magic. All of this goes into every bit of choreography in order to tell a good story.

A final note on safety I would like to address before you get started has to do with the equipment you use. Before I even start this section, let me just open with **I do not recommend ever using a retractable blade knife or dagger**, sometimes referred to as collapsible blade. These types of knives are very dangerous and can cause injury. I also believe that sharp knives never belong on set or in rehearsal. There have been occasions where a sharp knife was needed to cut an object onstage (bread, meat, etc.), but that knife was never used for combat, nor was it ever used to threaten a character. All combat weapons should have no cutting edge or sharp point. Many times, I have seen companies or choreographers use whatever is available, and all too often these knives and daggers were never meant for stage combat purposes. There are companies and prop makers out there who make theatrical knives and daggers, and there are places from which you can rent quality knives and daggers. A list of these companies can be found in Appendix B. There is also some great work being done by prop masters all over the world who are using wood, plastics, rubber, and aluminum to make believable but safe stage and screen weaponry. In all the exercises contained in this book, we always use rubber training knives, which can be acquired easily online from many companies at very affordable prices.

Partnering

If you are new to theatrical violence, the term 'partnering' may be foreign to you.

Working with a partner is a necessity in choreography. How you work with the individual or individuals is called partnering. Being a good partner is very important. Fights have a dialogue between the combatants, and it is this physical conversation that must play out to the audience. The physical, emotional, and visual elements are vital for dynamic choreography. Working together, you will manage the timing of the action, the intentions behind your character's actions and reactions, the emotions of gaining advantage and losing it, the points of focus, and the objectives of the moment.

Take care of yourself and your partner in the fight. Be aware constantly of how they are doing and how you are doing. Communicate openly with each other during rehearsals and check in regularly. Be safe.

Distance

The understanding of distance in theatrical combat is extremely important. We can look at distance in two ways when working choreography. The first is actors' distance, the space between two performers. The second is character distance, the space between two characters. Now these may sound like the same thing, but they are not. The actors can be out of distance from actually making contact with each other, but the characters can be in distance for an attack to happen, which will need a reaction from the other character. This stage distance is where most of our actions take place. We are selling the threat of danger to the audience but keeping the performers safe.

There are times when moves will be done in distance, so that the performers can make contact for actions like cuts, grabs, disarms, and other actions. However, with proper staging or camera angles, you can make stage distance look like the performers are close enough for actions to land and for the threat to be believable. There will be times when you want your characters to be out of distance from each other for actions like probing and false attacks or big sweeping gestures with the knife to keep the other character away from them.

Speed

I will talk a lot about speed and the speed of actions in this book. I always recommend learning an action slowly at first. Take your time, build your skill, and understand the action. Once you have mastered the technique and the choreography, you can bring it up to performance speed.

Performance speed is the pace at which the fight looks believable, the actions can be seen by the audience, and the actors have full control of their moves. Too fast, and the audience can't keep track of what is happening, and neither can your partner. Too slow, and the audience doesn't believe in the fight and is not buying the fact that the characters are in danger.

Tempo, the speed of the individual movements, must be controlled by the performers at all times. Some moves may be choreographed to be performed quickly, while others may be deliberately slow. This visible and audible variable creates the rhythm of the fight. If all the actions are rushed, or too slow, we lose this rhythm.

When working a fight, I always have performers 'walk through' the actions. Here they are just learning the choreography and are putting the moves together in a slow, controlled fashion. Once the performers have mastered the actions, reactions, sounds, and emotions of the scene, we will begin bringing it up to performance speed by moving it to half-speed. Half-speed has the performers flowing through the action as they would in the performance, combining all the elements together and finding the rhythm of the fight. Once half-speed is under full control, we will bump the tempo up to three-fourths speed. This is where the fight is just slightly slower than the performance speed. Here we start seeing the dynamics of the choreography taking its full shape in the space. Warning: This is also where performers may try to speed up, so be careful to keep the pace. After this is smooth and controlled, we will bring the fight up to performance speed. Here the moves should look natural and believable. Even a fight that is designed to look sloppy or messy is clearly seen and believed by the audience and the performers and keeps everyone safe.

Weapon Maintenance

A safe fight starts with safe equipment. As I stated earlier, no weapon should ever have a sharp edge or point. If you are using a real knife as a prop, you **must** grind down the edge and round off the point. When you grind down the edge of the knife, make sure it is not so flat that you now have two edges. Round off the corners of the grind to prevent cuts or tears to skin or clothing. There is never an excuse to put a person in real physical danger. Proper equipment must be used and maintained. Every rehearsal and performance should start and end with a prop check. Metal weapons can develop nicks and burrs along the edge that will need to be filed down. Wooden props may splinter or crack and need to be carefully inspected to prevent injury or weapon breakage. Hard plastic knives may also develop nicks or cracks along the blade. Spring-loaded blades, flip or tactical knives, or any knife that can open and close will need to be checked before and after use to make sure all parts are still functioning and have not been damaged.

I have found that the number-one cause for all equipment damage in a knife fight is repeated dropping of the knife. Very rarely will knives come in contact with another knife during a fight, but if they do, this is where additional damage to the blade can happen, especially nicks and burrs on the blade edge.

Always have one spare prop knife in case one gets damaged during a show run. **Never** use a damaged prop on stage.

3

HOLDING THE WEAPON AND STANCES

In knife fighting for the stage, there are several different methods for holding the knife or dagger. Looking back over historical material all the way through to modern training, many knives and daggers are designed to be used in very distinct ways, and their designs lend themselves to such use, while other knives are designed to be used in multiple ways and methods of fighting. Here we will look at the basic grips I have used most often in theatrical combat; I will explain their effectiveness and explore some of their variations.

Grip Energy

The first thing to develop when holding any weapon for the stage is proper grip, and this includes the amount of energy you put into holding your weapon. Many beginning students tend to hold the weapon very tightly, as in a 'death grip'. This grip is signaled by grabbing the handle

DOI: 10.4324/9781003147862-3

in the same way you would a hammer – with excessive energy applied to holding the weapons where the hand and forearm are extremely tense. This excess energy will hamper your use of the weapon on stage and cause your arm to tire out and be less controlled. In all the grips described in this chapter, you should maintain a relaxed grip, firm but soft. As Dale Girard says about holding a rapier in his book, *Actors on Guard*, it should be "cradled like a small bird: tight enough that it will not fly away, but not so tight that you will crush it" (Girard, 1997). Knife fighting is very fluid, and a relaxed grip will help you achieve this fluidity needed to create dynamic and exciting fights. Remember, this is not 'real' fighting for use on the streets but a choreographed dance of action between two or more performers.

Gripping the Weapon

Hammer/Fist Grip

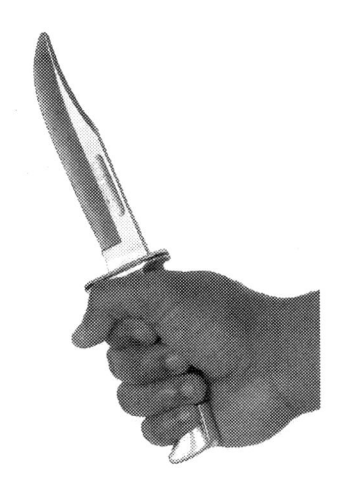

Figure 3.1 Hammer/Fist Grip

The most basic of all grips. This grip is achieved by grabbing the handle of the weapon, wrapping your fingers around the grip, and allowing the thumb to wrap over the index finger (see Figure 3.1). This is a good grip for stabbing and cutting while working with a large variation of hilt and handle styles. This grip can be used in **overarm** grip (see Figure 3.1), with the knife tip above the hand, or **underarm** grip (see Figure 3.4), with the knife tip below the hand, as in the *reverse grip*.

Saber Grip/Filipino Grip

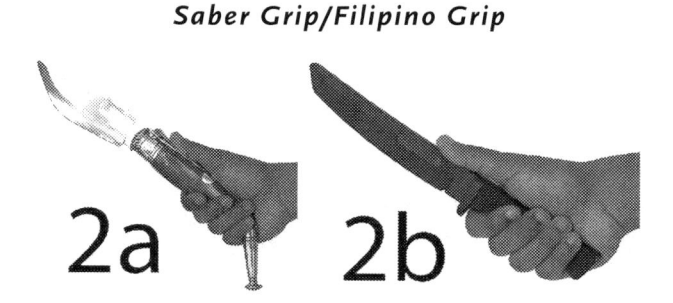

Figure 3.2 Saber Grip/Filipino Grip

The knife is held in an overarm grip. The hand is wrapped around the knife handle, while the thumb is placed on the top of either the handle for a saber grip (see Figure 3.2a), or the spine of the blade for a Filipino grip (see Figure 3.2b). When using an out-the-front automatic knife, pushing on the lever on the back of the handle will put the hand in a saber grip. These grips are good for strong point control and slashing styles of attacks. The Filipino grip is only useful on knives and daggers that do not have a cross-guard or hilt that prevents the thumb from extending down the back of the blade comfortably. For blades with a cross-guard or hilt, I recommend using the *side grip*.

Side Grip/Modified Saber Grip

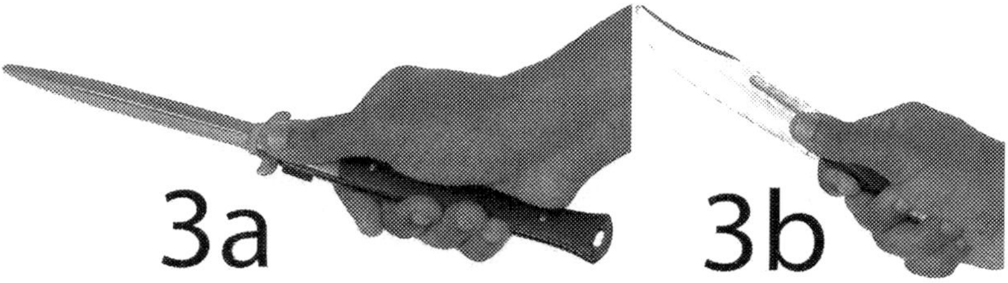

Figure 3.3 Side Grip/Modified Saber Grip

The knife is held in an overarm grip, as before, with the hand wrapped around the knife handle but with the thumb wedged against the side of the handle for a side grip (see Figure 3.3a), or on the flat of the blade for a modified saber grip (see Figure 3.3b). The side grip is common when using a switchblade knife; by grabbing lower on the handle and pressing the release button on the side of the handle, your natural grip ends up in the side grip. This grip is also the most common grip used on balisong/butterfly knives. The modified saber grip is quite common in the Spanish Navaja style of fighting. Spanish Navaja is the style I most often use when choreographing the knife fight in Bizet's *Carmen* between Escamillo and Don José. The modified saber grip can also be employed when using a parry dagger or main gauche in your non-sword hand – also known as "thumbing the blade". This is a good grip to use if your dagger will be coming into contact with another weapon that you need to have more control of, and it gives you good tip control of your dagger or knife. However, placing your thumb on the blade does expose it to attacks from weapons sliding down your blade.

Reverse Grip

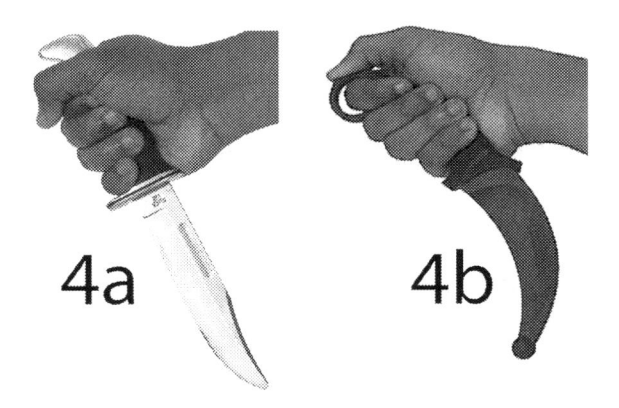

Figure 3.4 Reverse Grip

An underarm *hammer/fist* grip achieved by grabbing the handle of the weapon, tip facing down, wrapping your fingers around the grip, and allowing the thumb to wrap over the index finger (see Figure 3.4a). This grip is fine for all weapons with a hilt that will prevent your hand from slipping down the blade. However, if you are using a knife or dagger without a hilt, or with a small hilt, it is highly recommended that you use the *ice pick grip*.

The use of the reverse grip will require the performers to be closer in the fight than using the forward grip styles, as the reverse grip will take away distance in exchange for power. One of the most common knives used in the reverse grip is the karambit, an Indonesian knife with a curved handle and blade and a finger loop for the index finger at the base of the handle (see Figure 3.4b).

Ice Pick Grip

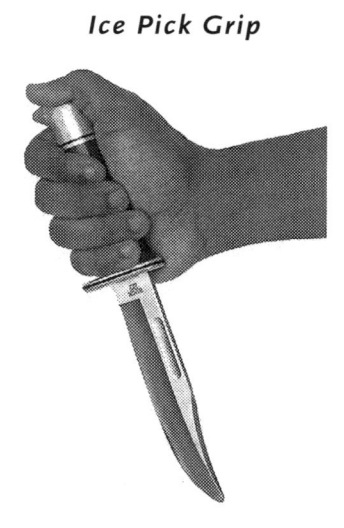

Figure 3.5 Ice Pick Grip

Holding the knife in an underarm reverse grip as before with the hand grabbing the handle of the weapon, tip facing down, wrapping your fingers around the grip. The change here is allowing the thumb to wrap over the top of the pommel or butt of the weapon, to keep the knife/dagger from slipping through your hand (see Figure 3.5).

Both the reverse and ice pick grips are well suited for traps, binds, and other actions explored later in the book.

Straight Razor Grip

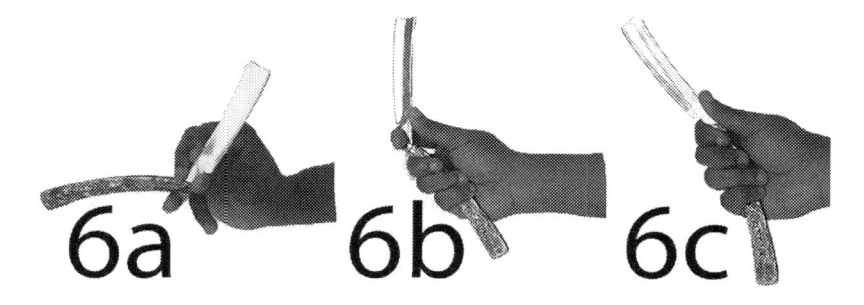

Figure 3.6 Straight Razor Grip

A. For self-shaving or slicing someone else's throat, as in *Sweeney Todd: The Demon Barber of Fleet Street*: Hold the blade edge in and the upper tang between your index finger and middle finger, while balancing the blade with your thumb. The backstrap of the razor will rest between your middle finger and ring finger, with your little finger supporting under the tang of the blade (see Figure 3.6a).

B. For fighting with the straight razor: Reverse the angle of the blade to edge out; now the backstrap will rest in your palm, and your ring finger will be under the hook of the tang and, along with your little finger, will rest on the backstrap (see Figure 3.6b).

C. Alternatively, you could also hold the razor in a saber grip, with your thumb on the back of the blade. However, due to no locking mechanism in the blade/handle, the body of the knife will wobble and shift around in your palm (see Figure 3.6c).

Stances

In this section, I will focus on the eight guard positions I have found to be most useful in telling a physical story on stage, although there are multiple variations of stances and guard positions used throughout history and around the world. Stances and guard positions are important for many reasons. In fighting, they are the ready stances for receiving or delivering attacks. They give the fighter an advantage or protection. In performance, they physically tell the story about the fighter and their state of mind. Do they know what they are doing? Are they a skilled fighter? Are they on the attack or are they staying completely defensive? These questions are answered by what kind of stance the performer is using and how they use it.

A note on right-handed versus left-handed: All stances will be described for performers with right-hand dominance. If you or someone you are working with is left-hand dominant, reverse/mirror the posture.

General points of attention:

- Keep your elbows in and close to your body; be careful of "chicken wings", or lifting your elbows to shoulder level.
- Keep your shoulders relaxed. Try to avoid excess tension in your arms and shoulders, as you want to be able to move your arms quickly and freely.

- Keep your knees bent and avoid locking your legs. There are many reasons to avoid locking your knees; however, in fighting, being able to move in any direction at any time requires you to keep your knees bent and your legs relaxed.
- Keep your hips, torso, and shoulders aligned towards your partner, although there will be instances and exceptions where this is changed for certain postures.
- Keep your body upright, and avoid hunching or leaning forward or backward.

The Basic On-Guard Stance

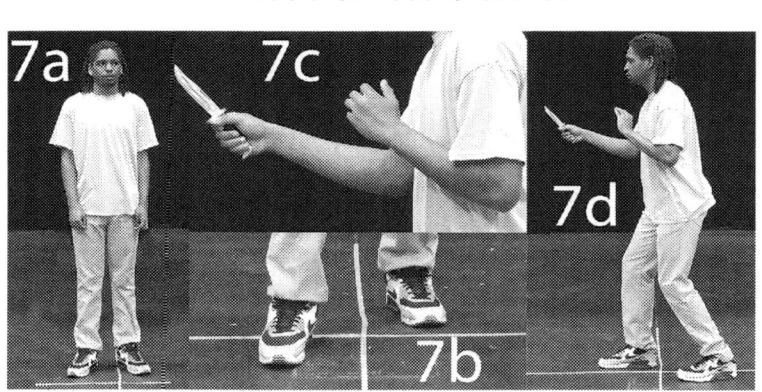

Figure 3.7 Basic On-Guard Stance

The most common stance we will use throughout this book is the basic on-guard stance. The performer starts by standing in a neutral position (see Figure 3.7a) with the knife in their right hand. Any grip will work, but for this exercise we will use the saber grip.

Feet & Legs: Open the feet a little wider than shoulder width and take a small step forward with the right foot. The heel of your right foot should be roughly in line with the tip of your left foot. Sink down into your stance to allow you to keep your knees soft and bent. Your right foot should be pointing towards your partner, and you can have a small turnout on your left foot (see Figure 3.7b).

Arms & Knife: In the basic on-guard stance, your hands will mirror your feet. Have the right hand about chest level and in front of your body, with the elbow bent and the knife pointed towards your partner. Your left hand will be raised to your chest level but closer to your body than the dominant knife hand. Keep your elbow bent and your left hand relaxed and open, palm down in pronation or slightly turned out to your partner (see Figure 3.7c).

Body: Your body should be relaxed, upright, and directly facing your partner. You may also have a very small shift in your torso towards your non-dominant side but be careful not to take yourself offline with your partner (see Figure 3.7d).

The Defensive On-Guard Stance

Figure 3.8 Defensive On-Guard Stance

The next stance we will explore is the defensive on-guard stance. This stance is similar to the basic on-guard stance but instead of stepping forward, the performer steps back. The performer starts by standing in a neutral position with the knife in their right hand (see Figure 3.8a).

Feet & Legs: Open the feet a little wider than shoulder width and take a small step backwards with the right foot. The heel of your left foot should be roughly in line with the tip of your right foot. Sink down into your stance to allow you to keep your knees soft and bent. Your left foot should be pointing towards your partner, and you can have a small turn-out on your right foot (see Figure 3.8b).

Arms & Knife: As in the basic on-guard stance, your hands will mirror your feet. Have the right hand about chest level and close in front of your body, with the elbow bent and the knife pointed towards your partner. Your left hand will be raised to your chest level but further from your body than the knife hand. Keep your elbow bent and your left hand relaxed and open, palm down in pronation or slightly turned out to your partner (see Figure 3.8c).

Body: Your body should be relaxed, upright, and directly facing your partner. In the defensive position, you may wish to exaggerate your trepidation by performing a small hunch forward. Be careful of overexaggeration of this posture. You may also have a very small shift in your torso towards your dominant side but be careful not to take yourself offline with your partner (see Figure 3.8d).

The Forward Linear Guard

Figure 3.9 Forward Linear Guard

The forward linear guard position can show that the performer is extremely aggressive or extremely nervous and unskilled. This is a forward extension guard with the knife held away from the body and the body leaning towards their partner.

Feet & Legs: Open the feet wider than shoulder width and take a medium-to-large step forward with the right foot. Sink down into your stance to allow you to keep your knees soft and bent. Your right foot should be pointing towards your partner, with a more pronounced turn-out on your left foot (see Figure 3.9a).

Arms & Knife: Have your right hand about chest level and fully extended in front of your body, with the elbow slightly bent and the knife pointed towards your partner. Your left hand will be raised to your chest level, closer to your body than the dominant knife hand but extended further from your body than in the basic on-guard position. Keep your elbow bent and your left hand relaxed and open, palm down in pronation or slightly turned out to your partner (see Figure 3.9b).

Body: Your body should be relaxed, leaning forward, and slightly turned towards your non-dominant side at about a 45-degree angle (see Figure 3.9c).

Points of Attention:

- Keep your right knee above your ankle, and do not allow your knee to go past your toes.
- Be careful not to overextend your stance, as you still need to be able to move in any direction without having to reset your feet or balance first.

The Defensive Linear Guard

Figure 3.10 Defensive Linear Guard

The defensive linear guard position can show that the performer is extremely defensive or that they are using an off-hand protective implement such as a towel, cloak, hat, or anything protecting the hand/forearm. This is a forward extension guard with the knife held close to the body, the defensive arm extended forward, and the body leaning away from their partner.

Feet & Legs: Open the feet wider than shoulder width and take a medium-to-large step backwards with the right foot. Sink down into your stance to allow you to keep your knees soft and bent. Your left foot should be pointing towards your partner, with a more pronounced turn-out on your right foot (see Figure 3.10a).

Arms & Knife: Have your left hand/arm at about chest level and extended in front of your body, with the elbow slightly bent. Your right hand will be raised to your chest level or can be held down at your waist but closer to your body. In the Spanish Navaja style of fighting, the knife is held in a side grip or modified saber grip with the thumb on the side of the blade, with the edge facing in or forward with your hand in supination (see Figure 3.10b).

Body: Your body should be relaxed, leaning slightly back, and slightly turned towards your dominant side at about a 45-degree angle (see Figure 3.10c).

The Low Front Guard

Figure 3.11 Low Front Guard

The low front guard position can show that the performer is aggressive and skilled. This is a forward guard with the knife held away from the body and the body leaning towards their partner.

Feet & Legs: Open the feet wider than shoulder width and take a medium step forward with the right foot. Sink down into your stance to allow you to keep your knees soft and bent. Your right foot should be pointing towards your partner, with a turnout on your left foot (see Figure 3.11a).

Arms & Knife: Have your right hand at about chest level and extended in front of your body, with the elbow sharply bent and the knife pointed towards your left if in saber or hammer grip or towards your right if in reverse grip. Your left hand will be raised to your chest level, at the same level as your knife hand but closer to your body than the dominant knife hand, and it will be kept close to your body. Keep your elbow bent and your left hand relaxed and open, palm down in pronation (see Figure 3.11b).

Body: Your body should be relaxed, with a strong bend forward, and slightly turned towards your dominant side but still focused on your partner.

The Low Back Guard

Figure 3.12 Low Back Guard

The low back guard position can show that the performer is extremely defensive and skilled. This is a back guard with the knife held away from the body and the body leaning towards their partner.

Feet & Legs: Open the feet wider than shoulder width and take a medium step forward with the left foot. Sink down into your stance to allow you to keep your knees soft and bent. Your left foot should be pointing towards your partner, with a slight turnout on your right foot (see Figure 3.12a).

Arms & Knife: Have your right hand at about waist level and partially extended in front of your body, with the elbow bent and the knife pointed towards your partner. Your left hand will be either at knife level or raised above your waist to your chest level but further from your body than the dominant knife hand. Keep your elbow bent and your left hand relaxed and open, palm down in pronation or slightly turned out to your partner (see Figure 3.12b).

Body: Your body should be relaxed with a slight lean forward and slightly turned towards your non-dominant side at about a 45-degree angle, weight resting more on your back leg.

The Hidden Guard

Figure 3.13 Hidden Guard

The hidden guard position can show that the performer is sneaky and trying to hide the fact they have a weapon. This is a neutral guard with the knife out of sight of their partner (see Figure 3.13).

Feet & Legs: The body can be in almost any position, though a forward-facing neutral stance is most common. There is no leaning, and the feet are in a natural standing position.

Arms & Knife: Arms should be totally relaxed, not holding any tension in this position. The knife can be held in reverse grip, tucked up against the forearm, behind the performer. Another variation can be with the arms crossed behind the back, the knife hidden behind the back or buttocks. Yet another variation can be with the body turned out and the left side forward, the knife held in a hammer or saber grip and tucked against the right thigh, out of view from their partner.

Body: Your body should be relaxed and in a neutral position.

Points of Attention:

- This guard comes in many different varieties, but the most important element to remember is that the knife should be hidden from the partner and visible to the audience at some point.
- The body and energy should be neutral, with neither an aggressive nor defensive posturing.

The 'Boxers' Guard

Figure 3.14 Boxers Guard

The boxers guard position can show that the performer is aggressive or defensive. This is a guard that mimics the Western boxing guard position, with the knees bent and arms up protecting the upper torso – like the reverse on-guard position but with the arms closer in and the feet closer together (see Figure 3.14).

Feet & Legs: Open the feet to shoulder width and take a small step forward with the left foot. Sink down into your stance to allow you to keep your knees soft and bent. Your left foot should be pointing towards your partner, with a very slight turnout on your right foot.

Arms & Knife: Have your right hand at about shoulder level and pulled in close to your body, with the elbow sharply bent and the knife pointed up if in a variation of the saber grip or pointed down if in a reverse grip. Your left hand will be raised to your shoulder level and slightly further from your body than the dominant knife hand. Keep your elbow bent and your left hand relaxed and open, palm down in pronation or in a loose fist. Both the knife hand and open hand should be closer to your center line and not as open as in the basic on-guard position.

Body: Your body should be relaxed, straight, and in line towards your partner. Your chin should be tucked down and your eyes focused forward.

Variation: You can switch this position by swapping the right and left side, so that the left leg and empty hand are back and the right leg and knife hand are forward.

Point of Attention:

- Keep your arms and hands in close to your center line and avoid a wide stance. It is very easy to be too relaxed in this position and open into a basic on-guard stance.

Closing Comments

The previously described grips and guard positions are the ones I use the most often in choreographies. I find that they can tell the story of the characters and the fight quickly and are easy for performers to learn and utilize in a timely fashion. Of course, there are many different styles of grips and guards and an almost endless list of variations on all of them, so picking the right ones will always depend on the story you are trying to tell.

A great example of guards and grips telling a story is in Quentin Tarantino's *Kill Bill: Vol.* 1 (Miramax Films, 2003, Fight Choreographer: Rob Moses. Zoë Bell, stunt double: The Bride; Angela Meryl, stunt double: Vernita). In the knife fight scene in Vernita Green's living room, The Bride (Uma Thurman) and Vernita (Vivica A. Fox) come to a moment in the fight when each one is waiting for an opening as a school bus pulls up to the front of the house. In this shot, we see both actors framed in the window: Vernita in a forward guard position, holding the knife in a modified saber grip with the index finger extended along the flat of the blade, and The Bride in a defensive guard position, holding her knife in a reverse grip. With the physical action of Vernita leaning forward and The Bride in a slight lean back, we are being told a very clear story in this one moment of fighting.

4

FOOTWORK AND BODY DYNAMICS

Now that you have explored the various types of grips and guards, you will move into footwork. Footwork is literally and figuratively the foundation of all knife fighting, and to be honest, of all fighting systems. To quote Payson Burt, "no matter how many systems there were in the world, that the human body is made a certain way and that those limitations are the common thread that binds every system of movement together" (Burt, 1993). Moving your body starts with moving your feet. Proper footwork helps guarantee that fights are dynamic, your alignment is correct, and that you can easily move in and out to perform any action that is needed in the choreography.

A note on terminology: I will often refer to the **line of engagement** throughout this book, and that term can be confusing at times. Payson Burt defined this best as "an imaginary line that represents the shortest distance between two combatants" (Burt, 1993). Basically, this is the line in which the weapon is threatening and that action can transpire upon

DOI: 10.4324/9781003147862-4

during the fight. This imaginary line is usually directly in front of you and connecting you to your partner while you are on-guard. As fighters move around, they can become **offline** (an action consisting of taking the body or weapon off the line of engagement) or stay **online** (an action consisting of keeping the body or weapon on the line of engagement).

Using the Box

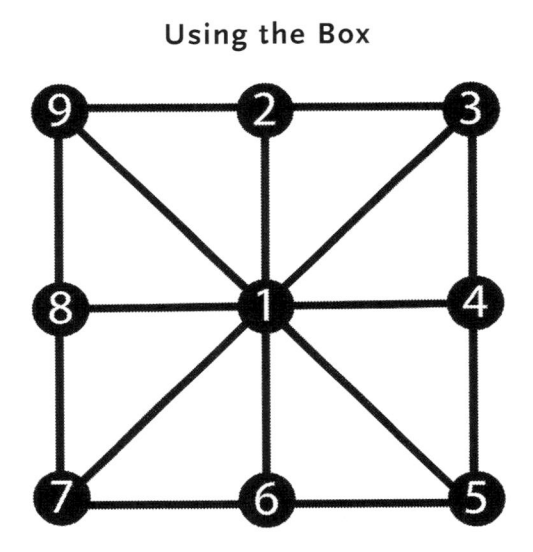

Figure 4.1 Footwork Box

The "box" is an imaginary set of lines that your feet will move along during a fight. Practicing footwork within the box is a great training tool, as it helps performers develop coordination between body and feet and makes fights more dynamic and active (see Figure 4.1).

The areas of the box are as follows:

1. Center
2. Forward Center
3. Forward Right Corner
4. Right Center
5. Back Right Corner
6. Back Center

7. Back Left Corner
8. Left Center
9. Forward Left Corner

General Points of Attention:

- All footwork described will start in the basic on-guard stance, with right foot leading.
- All footwork can be mirrored with the left foot leading.
- Keep your body relaxed while you are focused on your feet; do not let tension build up in other areas, such as your shoulders.
- Let the feet, not the torso, lead the way of your movement. Moving your torso first may cause balance issues.
- Keep your knees bent and make your movement fluid. You do not want to rock back and forth or side to side as you move due to repeated weight shifts.

Straight Steps

Straight steps can be either simple or compound footwork actions used to close, gain, or maintain distance between two performers while maintaining forward direction without pivoting or turning of the body. They are basic movements that are easy to learn and execute in any space requirements or restrictions.

Straight Step

The straight step is a simple step action completed either forward or backward without a recovery step.

Forward: Move your lead foot to forward center, shifting your weight 60/40 in favor of your lead foot.

Backward: Move your lag foot to back center, shifting your weight 60/40 in favor of your lag foot.

Switch Step

A switch step is a compound footwork action that helps you adjust your footwork for any action you may want to do by replacing your lead or lag leg with the other leg. This step can be done in any guard position, but for this exercise we will start in the basic on-guard stance and move into the defensive on-guard stance.

Starting in basic on-guard with your right foot forward and left foot back, step forward with your left foot, in line with your right foot but equal distance apart, and then quickly step back with your right foot, equal distance back that the left foot moved forward. You should now be in the defensive on-guard stance with your left foot forward.

Advance

The advance is a compound straight step forward followed by a recovery step forward with the lag foot.

You should finish with your feet on-guard and the same distance apart as when you started.

Retreat

The retreat is a compound straight step back followed by a recovery step backward with the lead foot.

You should finish with your feet on-guard and the same distance apart as when you started.

Sidestep

Sidesteps will quickly move you right or left. An area to focus on is to make sure your feet end in your on-guard stance at the same distance apart as when they started. Another area to pay attention to is shifting your weight to allow the movement but not letting your upper body wobble as you do the move.

Right: Step straight to the right with your right foot, followed by a recovery into your on-guard position with your left foot.

Left: Step straight to the left with your left foot, followed by a recovery into your on-guard position with your right foot.

Passing Steps

The straight passing step is a simple passing step to move either forward or backward by shifting which foot is in the lead position and allowing the other foot to pivot slightly.

To pass forward: Move the lag foot forward and allow the new lag foot to pivot slightly to adjust to on-guard.

To pass backwards: Move the lead foot backward; the new lead foot will pivot to point forward while the new lag foot will pivot to adjust to on-guard.

Shuffle and Skip Steps

A quick and easy way to add a unique dynamic to a fight is to include the use of shuffle and skip steps. This compound action can make it seem as if the performers are moving more than they are in the space. This can be helpful if you need a small space to feel bigger. These moves can also add personality to the fight. These quick actions can make a character seem overly cautious/apprehensive, or aggressive/antagonistic. Another use I have found for these quick action steps is in opera choreography where I need the performers to move with the rhythm and energy of the music. These quick actions make the fight look faster than it is, where I don't want to speed up the actions but to make it look like the performers are high energy. I will also combine this with arm/knife movements that I will cover later in the book.

Straight Shuffle Steps

The shuffle step is a piece of compound footwork that can move you forward, backward, or sideways quickly. An area to focus on in this movement is to move quickly but make sure that one foot lands before the other foot moves. Another area to pay attention to is to make sure you do not cross your steps, as they should not pass the other foot in the movement.

Forward and backward shuffle steps: Starting with your right foot forward in the on-guard stance, bring your left foot straight forward, parallel to your right foot, and step forward with your right foot quickly to move into your on-guard position. To move backward, just reverse the previous actions starting with your right foot.

Sideways shuffle steps: Starting with your right foot forward in the on-guard stance, bring your left foot straight towards your center line, toes almost touching the heel of your right foot. Immediately move your right foot straight to the right, returning to on-guard and maintaining the same distance as your on-guard stance. To move to the left, just reverse this process, moving your right foot first.

Straight Skip Steps

Skip steps are ways to move quickly with a spring-like action in any direction, like a shuffle step. However, unlike the shuffle step, the skip step replaces the lead or lag foot on transition as opposed to stepping beside it. The trick to this step is to be on the balls of your feet; this helps the bounce-like skip action that allows the feet to change.

Forward or backward: Starting with your right foot forward in the on-guard stance, bring your left foot straight forward, parallel to your right foot. As that foot lands, immediately skip forward with your right foot quickly to move into your on-guard position. To move backward, just reverse the previous actions, starting with your right foot.

Sideways: Starting with your right foot forward in the on-guard stance, bring your left foot straight towards your center line. Immediately skip your right foot straight to the right, returning to on-guard and maintaining the same distance as your on-guard stance. To move to the left, just reverse this process, moving your right foot first.

Displacements

The displacement is a simple footwork action consisting of a single step with either the right or left foot, and it is used to quickly take yourself away from an attack. These actions can be combined with full-body leans to add an additional dynamic element to a scene.

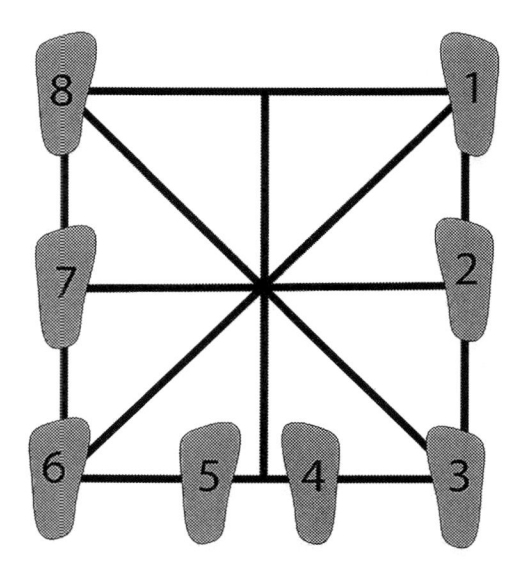

Figure 4.2 Footwork Box With Displacements

Displacements work by moving one foot, usually the foot closest to the direction you are moving, to one of four locations in the box. The right foot can move to either Forward Right Corner (1), Right Center (2), Back Right Corner (3), or Back Center (4), while the left foot can move to either Forward Left Corner (8), Left Center (7), Back Left Corner (6), or Back Center (5) (see Figure 4.2). Notice that there is a difference between Back Center 4 and 5. Be careful not to end up in a narrow/linear stance that lacks balance. Allow the foot to move directly back along a straight line.

Angled/Diagonal Steps

The angled/diagonal steps are the same as a straight step except that they are performed at a 45-degree angle, as it moves from your center position to any of the corners of the box. These are good moves to close distance (forward) or gain distance (backward), or to keep pace with your partner who is also performing an angled step.

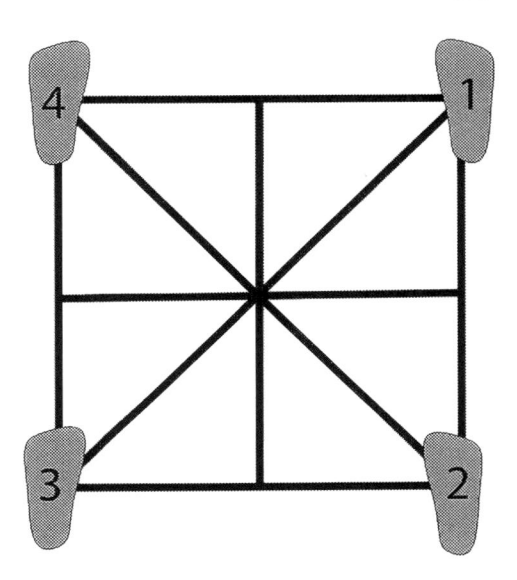

Figure 4.3 Angled/Diagonal Steps

In these variations, steps can move to the Forward Right Corner (1), Back Right Corner (2), Back Left Corner (3), or the Forward Left Corner (4) (see Figure 4.3).

The trick to the angled/diagonal steps is the same as with displacements, in that you always want to lead with the foot in the direction you are going. If you are moving to the right, move the right foot first, whether it is in the lead or lag position. The same goes for moving to the left — move the left foot first.

Unless your partner is keeping pace with you, you will need to pivot your stance at the end of the move to keep online with your partner.

Pivot Steps

Pivot steps can quickly allow you to avoid attacks or realign you with your partner during an action. These steps are quick actions that can pivot you either 90 or 180 degrees and can be performed from any guard position. The main trick to the pivot step is to be on the ball of your pivot foot and to not keep your foot flat as you move. Once the move is finished, flatten your feet into the on-guard position. Pivot steps are also known as slips, demi-voltes, and voltes.

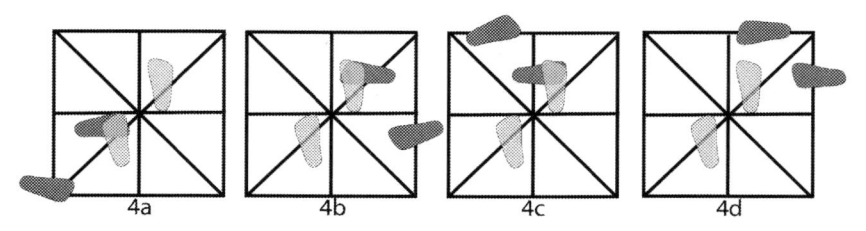

Figure 4.4 Pivot Steps

90-Degree Pivot Steps

In this step, we are going to assume that the character needs to pivot 90 degrees to engage their opponent because they moved quickly to one side or that the other character is charging with an attack and the character needs to avoid the action.

Pivot back right: From your on-guard stance, right foot forward, pivoting on your left foot, swing your right foot back and around as your torso turns 90 degrees to the right (see Figure 4.4a).

Pivot back left: From your on-guard stance, right foot forward, pivoting on your right foot, swing your left foot back and around as your torso turns 90 degrees to the left (see Figure 4.4b).

Pivot forward right: From your on-guard stance, step forward with your left foot in a passing step. Pivot on the balls of both feet to allow your torso to turn right 90 degrees (see Figure 4.4c).

Pivot forward left: From your on-guard stance, step forward with your right foot; then, pivoting on your right foot, like the pivot back left, swing your left foot back and around as your torso turns 90 degrees to the left (see Figure 4.4d).

Pay attention to your feet, and make sure you are not ending up in a linear stance. You should still be in a well-balanced stance.

180-Degree Pivot Steps

With this step, we are assuming that our character in the choreography needs to turn around 180 degrees. This may be because their opponent has managed to get behind them or because the character has passed their opponent and needs to turn and face them. With knife fighting always being in close quarters, the opportunity to pass behind or around your partner can happen quite often.

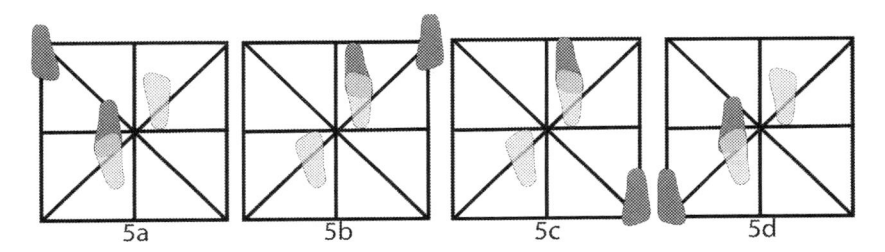

Figure 4.5 180-Degree Pivot Steps

Pivot 180 back right: Starting in on-guard, right foot forward, step with your right foot back and around to Forward Left Corner. Allow your hips and torso to turn 180 degrees to your right by staying on the ball of your left foot as you turn. You will end with your left foot forward and your right foot back (see Figure 4.5a).

Pivot 180 back left: Starting in on-guard, right foot forward, step with your left foot back and around to Forward Right Corner. Allow your hips and torso to turn 180 degrees to your left by staying on the ball of your right foot as you turn. You will end with your right foot forward and your left foot back (see Figure 4.5b).

Pivot 180 forward right: Starting in on-guard, right foot forward, step with your left foot forward and around to Back Right Corner. Allow your hips and torso to turn 180 degrees to your right by staying on the ball of your right foot as you turn. You will end with your left foot forward and your right foot back (see Figure 4.5c).

Pivot 180 forward left: Starting in on-guard, right foot forward, step with your right foot forward and around to Back Left Corner. Allow your hips and torso to turn 180 degrees to your left by staying on the ball of your left foot as you turn. You will end with your right foot forward and your left foot back (see Figure 4.5d).

C-Steps

The C-step is a passing forward or backward action, but the passing foot swings in close to the planted foot. This footwork can be used to create more dynamic and energetic movements in your choreography. The C-step also can be used to close or gain distance between you and your partner or can be part of the natural ebb and flow of the choreography.

Body Dynamics

Although footwork can add a level of excitement and realism to choreography, we still need to continue telling the story of the fight with our upper body. This is where I see a lot of choreography fall short. There are many elements that can cause choreography to lack energy, such as actors' nerves, if they are 100% focused on the blade work and not paying attention to their body work; or lacking movement, where the two combatants are just facing each other, squared up, and throwing knife attacks. The body dynamics and intent of any fight help accentuate the story being told and help the audience stay engaged with the fight.

One of my top recommendations is to start adding in body dynamics as you are doing footwork drills, and let them become just as much as your habit as good, strong footwork.

Bobbing

Bobbing is one of the vertical actions of upper body work that allows the head to drop under an attack and keeps the body moving and harder to hit. You see this a lot in boxing, along with weaving.

One thing to watch out for when bobbing is not to just lean forward. With bobbing, you want to squat down, using your knees and keeping your shoulders over your hips.

Weaving

Weaving is the action of moving horizontally, or side to side and backward, taking your upper torso and head offline of an attack, and it is often combined with the bobbing action. Weaving can also include a twist of your torso during the action.

Crouching

Crouching down, another of the vertical actions, allows the combatant to either completely evade a high-line target or drop down to attack a low-line target. When crouching, it is important to remember to keep your shoulders above your hips and not just lean forward with the action.

Active Hands

Active hands are something that can make or break a fight. Too much hand action is just confusing and pointless; no hand action at all keeps the situation from looking engaging or threatening. The right use of active hands is to be found in the choreography, the character, and the performer's personal style.

To practice active hands, you can start with small actions between your attacks and defenses:

- Let your weapon and non-weapon hands do small circles in the air in front of your chest. Keeping the knife and the empty hand moving, even in small actions like this, adds a level of dynamics to the fight.
- Let the knife hand and empty hand trade places while walking and switching guard positions.
- Change the level of your hands. Bring your knife higher and your empty hand lower, and vice versa.
- Throw short fake actions, using either the knife hand or the empty hand to throw short fake attacks.
- If the character is unskilled, allow them to hold the knife with both hands and have a bit of shake to the knife, showing they are scared or nervous.
- Although I do not recommend this one very often, you could change grips while moving around. Go from saber grip to ice pick grip, then

back to hammer grip. The reason I do not recommend this is that it is usually overused, and in live performances, actors – in a moment of stage adrenaline – tend to drop the knife or let it spin out of their hand.

Drills

Drills are a great way to warm up performers and set the actions into muscle memory. The following drills are recommendations for simple warm-up exercises, though any combination can be performed as a drill. I highly recommend that you play with the following but also come up with your own combos and drills.

The Simple Box

The simple box drill is a nice warm-up to get your legs moving and to practice the basics.

Start in basic on-guard, then advance forward, sidestep left, retreat, and finish with a sidestep right. You are now back in your original spot.

Variations can include any combination of moves in any direction. Explore making different shapes with your movement. Another variation is to include shuffle and skip steps.

The Triangle Drill

The triangle is one of the basic combinations of footwork drills that I personally use in my own warm-ups and when working with performers.

The forward triangle: Starting from a basic on-guard position in the middle of your box, you will angle step forward right at a 45-degree angle to the forward right corner of your box. Then sidestep left to the forward left corner, followed by an angle step back right, returning you to your original starting position.

The backward triangle: Starting from a basic on-guard position in the middle of your box, you will angle step back right at a 45-degree angle to the back right corner of your box. Then sidestep left to the back left corner, followed by an angle step forward right, returning you to your original starting position.

Variations can include the use of shuffle steps or skip steps. You can also start moving left first. These can be combined or done separately. Another fun variation is to work this drill in different guard positions.

The Ranging Star

The ranging star is a drill for stepping out into the six points of your box with displacement steps.

Starting clockwise, start in the middle of your box in basic on-guard. Step with your right foot to the forward right corner, then return to on-guard. Continue this process by stepping out to center right, the back right corner, and finally back center. Switching to your left foot, step to back center, back left corner, center left, and finally forward left corner. Remember to return to on-guard between steps.

Variations include changing directions to counterclockwise and changing your guard stance.

The Diamond

The diamond drill works both the forward and reverse angles of footwork. This drill is also beneficial for remembering that the box is always moving with your footwork.

Start in the center of your box in right foot forward on-guard. Using an angled step, move to the forward right corner. This is now your new center position. As each step happens, reset your center. Continue this drill by moving to the forward left corner, to the back left corner, then finishing with moving to the back right corner. You should be back at your original starting point.

Variation can include mixing this drill up both clockwise and counterclockwise. Another variation is to do the diamond on the horizontal axis: start with forward right corner, then back right corner, back left corner, then forward left corner to return to your starting position. This variation can also be changed up both clockwise and counterclockwise.

Still another variation is to start at the top of the diamond as opposed to the bottom, so that your first step is a back corner step. The top and bottom diamonds can be linked, just as the left and right diamonds can be linked together.

Closing Comments

As I stated at the beginning of this chapter, footwork is the foundation upon which choreography is built. In films, we don't usually get to see much of the footwork the fighters are doing, unless it involves a kick, knee, or a knee slam into the knife – such as the one used in *John Wick: Chapter 2*. In the subway fight between John Wick (Keanu Reeves) and Cassian (Common), the camera stays focused above the waist for most of the fight. However, focus does shift to the feet/legs when they are doing a unique action such as kicking, kneeing, or assisting a stab. Many films keep the shots close and tight during knife fights; in theatre, we do not get that ability. Live fights in theatre or opera are on full-body display to the audience. This is where footwork will really come to play a major factor in the choreography. As an actor, it is easy to get too focused on one aspect of the fight, such as footwork or building dynamics into the action, but remember to keep the focus on the characters and the fighting.

5

BASIC ATTACKS

Attacks with the knife are usually quick actions, and due to their intimacy and quickness, it is often easier to track the actions and micro-actions in film than it is on stage. In film, we can zoom in and frame the fighters to easily see the actions better, whereas on stage, the audience is farther back and the actions must be bigger, more pronounced, and slowed down so that the audience can see the action happening. This can sometimes lead to people in the audience feeling that the fight is fake, unrealistic, or lacking intent, and the same is true when live theatre techniques are used in film. And they are right – these moves are fake and unrealistic. We do not want to have even the slightest chance of our actors or audience getting hurt. However, with the right techniques and proper staging, even a theatrical knife fight can look as good as a

DOI: 10.4324/9781003147862-5

filmed knife fight. These techniques will be discussed in more depth later in the book, but for now, let us explore the basic offensive action of the knife.

A note on terminology: In reference to **distance**, the space between the performers, I will refer to performers and attacks that are **in distance** (when the distance between two individuals is close enough for the weapon or action to make contact without taking a step) and **out of distance** (when the distance between two individuals is far enough apart that a weapon or action cannot make contact without stepping towards their partner). Due to the nature of knife fighting, most of the time the actions are done in distance with proper safety protocols in place. For more information on distance, see the opening chapter on safety. Another term I will use is **target/targeting,** the area of the body at which the attack or action is aimed. When talking about targeting, I will also be referencing the **lines of attack**. The lines of attack refer to the imaginary planes that bisect the body into four equal sections – one vertical, defining the inside line (non-weapon side) and the outside line (weapon bearing side), and one horizontal, defining the high line (above the waist) and the low line (below the waist) (see Figure 5.1b).

The Cutting Actions

Like most edged weapons, the knife follows the basic eight-angle diagram. This diagram will be explored next in more detail. For now, an important technique to focus on is to always lead your cuts with the edge of your knife; on a double-bladed dagger, this would be the **true edge**, the edge of the blade that is aligned with the middle knuckles (the joint between the proximal and intermediate phalanges) of the hand holding it. Another thing to be careful of is to not twist your wrist halfway through the action and take your edge away from the target.

The Basic Cutting Actions

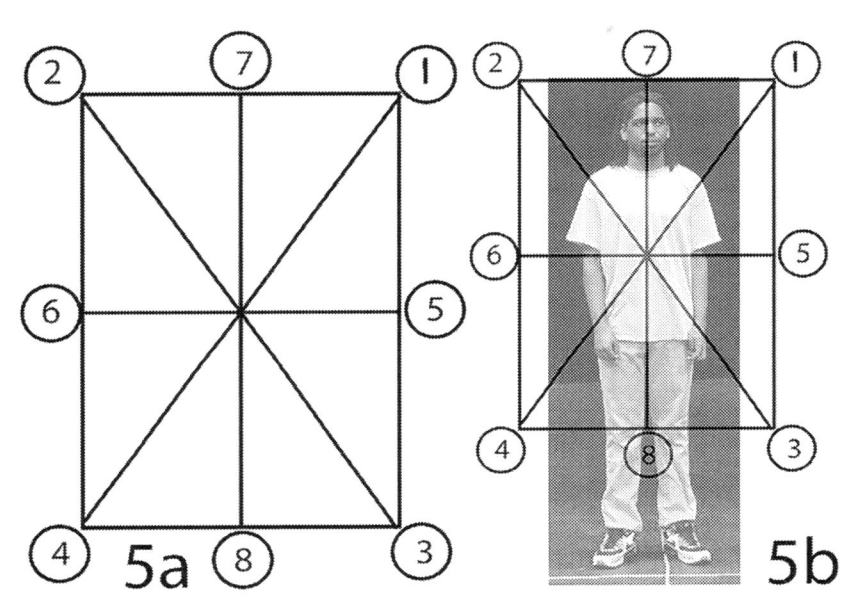

Figure 5.1 Eight-Angle Cutting Diagram

In Figure 5.1a, I have laid out the basic eight-angle diagram of the cutting lines. Like the box we create for our feet, this diagram for our attacking actions will constantly be in motion according to your target. You can start with the big picture of imagining this diagram set on top of the full body of your partner (see Figure 5.1b). The basic cuts start with four diagonal cuts, starting with downward diagonals, from the left shoulder down to the right hip (1) and from the right shoulder down to the left hip (2); next we move to upward diagonals, from the left hip up to the right shoulder (3) and from the right hip up to the left shoulder (4). Next are the two horizontal cuts, from their left to right (5) and from their right to left (6), and although we can put these cuts anywhere on the body, we are starting with targeting the stomach/abdomen area. Finally, the basic cuts end with the two vertical cuts, down (7) and then up (8).

The techniques I describe here are performed out of distance, in saber grip, and are presented from the perspective of a right-handed performer without the weapon coming into contact with the partner's body. If you or your partner is left-handed, the actions should be mirrored.

For beginning knife fighters, I like to begin with the performer exaggerating their actions by having the cut start about 8 to 10 inches outside their partner's body, then slowly cutting all the way through the body, stopping about 8 to 10 inches outside the body. The reason I do this is that I have found, for performers without any prior theatrical combat experience, it helps them relax by not actually threatening their partner or being threatened and helps remove some of the tension they want to incorporate into their knife arm. As a director and fight choreographer, I have found that some actors may have some negative experiences in their past, which may deal with knives or being threatened. We should never just assume that a performer is fine with being threatened by a weapon. Take the time at the beginning to check in with your performers, letting them know what actions will be done and walk them through how the actions will be done. Even in productions like opera, where there is extremely limited time to train and choreograph the performers, taking the time to do this at the beginning is very beneficial for the mental health of your performers. I will continue talking about these issues throughout the book.

Working the Basic Cuts

The cuts are named according to how they are performed and explained with the body of the partner. Starting from the basic on-guard position, extend your knife arm out while pointing the tip towards the target, about 8 to 10 inches from the body, and then begin your cut while leading with the edge of your blade, moving through the body and returning to on-guard after the action. The goal of these exercises is to develop the angles of attack in the cuts. Later in this chapter, I will talk about incorporating flow and body dynamics to these actions. As the skill level of the performer increases, all of these cuts can be altered depending on your character's skill level. The cutting actions can be the large, slashing actions of an unskilled fighter or the tight, strategic cuts of a trained professional.

Diagonal High Right to Low Left Cut

This descending cut moves at a 45-degree angle down and across the body. The cut starts outside your partner's left shoulder, moves through the body, and ends outside their right hip.

Diagonal High Left to Low Right Cut

This second descending cut moves at a 45-degree angle down and across the body. The cut starts outside your partner's right shoulder, moves through the body, and ends outside their left hip.

Diagonal Low Right to High Left Cut

This ascending cut moves at a 45-degree angle up and across the body. The cut starts outside your partner's left hip, moves up through the body, and ends outside their right shoulder.

Diagonal Low Left to High Right Cut

This second ascending cut moves at a 45-degree angle up and across the body on the opposite line. The cut starts outside your partner's right hip, moves up through the body, and ends outside their left shoulder.

Horizontal Cut Right to Left

This cut moves in a flat horizontal action across the body. The cut is supinated (palm up) and moves from outside your partner's left side, across the body, and ends outside on their right side.

Horizontal Cut Left to Right

This cut moves in a flat horizontal action across the body. The cut is pronated (palm down) and moves from outside your partner's right side, across the body, and ends outside on their left side.

Vertical Cut Down

The seventh action is the vertical cut from high line to low line. Even with the performers being out of distance, we do not want the tip or edge of the blade moving anywhere near the face, so for this exercise we will target the shoulders on the downward cut. The cut moves from above your partner's body/target and moves vertically down through the body/target.

Vertical Cut Up

The last action of the cut diagram is the vertical cut from low line to high line. This cut can be tricky with a knife in saber grip, so focus on the action going from hip to shoulder on the same side in a straight line. This cut is used frequently when your knife is held in reverse/ice pick grip with true edge forward, and it works beautifully when combined with a reverse grip and a karambit knife. There are two options for doing this cut with a knife in saber grip.

The first option is a modified diagonal low right to high left cut, where instead of cutting diagonally you move the angle straight up the left side of your partner's body.

The second option is a modified diagonal low left to high right cut, where instead of cutting diagonally you move the angle straight up the right side of your partner's body.

If the knife is in reverse grip, move the knife straight up the target, leading with the true edge of your blade.

Basic Stabbing Actions

The next action in fighting with knives and daggers that we will explore is the basic stabbing actions. Though maybe not as flashy as cuts and swipes, stabs and thrusts have their place in some amazingly dynamic choreography. For example, in the hallway fight scene in Repo Men (Universal Films 2010, Miguel Spochnik: Director, Hiro Koda: Choreographer), Remy (Jude Law) makes his way down a hallway of attackers. This scene shows some beautiful knife work, including a double stab down from behind and one of my favorite moves, a stab to the foot. And what would Shakespeare's *Julius Caesar* be without stabs and thrusts?

A note on hand positions: The beautiful thing about stabs and thrusts is that these actions can come from anywhere (high, low, mid-line, forward, sideways, and even backward) and target any part of the body within reach, even the foot. However, to simplify the learning process, I will examine what I have come to find as the four most basic styles of stabs and thrusts. Simplifying the stabs down helps keep beginning performers from getting overwhelmed with too much information or technical jargon, and beautiful choreography does not have to be full of complicated moves. Although I am using terms such as **pronated** (the position of the hand with the palm facing down), **supinated** (the position of the hand with the palm facing up), and **half-pronation/supination** (the position of the hand with the thumb either pointed up and the palm facing the inside, or the thumb pointed down with the palm facing the outside), they are being used as a beginning reference for learning the basic actions. Like the cutting exercises earlier, the stabs will be practiced out of distance and will <u>not</u> make contact with your partner.

The Forward Stab

The first stab is a forward action with the knife held in an overhand grip and the hand typically in half-pronation and directed forward towards the target.

The Forehand Stab

With the knife held in overhand grip and the hand pronated, this stab can be delivered directly forward or from the attacker's right side from almost any angle.

The Backhand Stab

When the knife is held in an overhand grip with the hand supinated, this stab can be delivered directly forward or from the attacker's left side.

The Underhand Stab

With the knife held in an underhand grip, this stab can be delivered to any area of the body.

A great example of this is your classic horror-film-style stab from above. Probably the most legendary stab in horror films is from Alfred Hitchcock's *Psycho*. In the famous shower scene, we "see" Marion Crane (Janet Leigh) stabbed multiple times by a shadowy figure holding a kitchen knife in the underhand grip with the edge facing in. This is a beautiful example of implied violence, which I will talk more about later in the book. Unlike the implied violence of *Psycho*, the slow penetration of a bayonet shows the audience the gritty realism of war in Steven Spielberg's *Saving Private Ryan*, when Private Mellish (Adam Goldberg) is stabbed by a German soldier (Mac Steinmeier). This is another great example in cinema of an underhand stab. For a humorous take on the underhand stab, we can look to Marvel's *Guardians of the Galaxy Vol. 2*, when Drax (Dave Bautista) cuts through the Abilisk from the inside, using multiple stabs while yelling.

The Cut Drills

I have found that cut drills are wonderful ways to develop flow and smoothness with a performer's actions. They can be as simple as just moving the hand/knife through the air or as complex as full-body movements while working breath control. In this section, we will start with just the simple introductory drills and work towards full-body dynamic drills. One of the things to remember about these drills is although we are applying them to the entire body of our partner, they can be narrowed down to an extended limb or they can move around the body as the performer moves around.

As before, these drills will be learned out of distance so that no contact is being made between the performers. In the next chapter, we will start exploring blocks and checks. In those exercises, performers will start working the knife drills in distance. It is highly recommended to have a solid understanding of the following drills and a smooth and controlled technique before moving to partnered blocks and checks.

The Basic 10-Point Drill

Many martial art systems like Escrima, Kali, Pencak Silat, Systema, Tantōjutsu, and other systems of knife fighting use a set and defined method for training students in their respective tradition. While all these systems have great merit and different advantages, here we will use a basic 10-point attack system with an overhand grip and develop our own version of a flow. The point of these exercises is to create a system that can adapt to any choreography in which it is applied while still allowing room for stylistic changes that the story, scene, or character needs. Although these drills are written for the perspective of a right-handed individual, left-handed individuals can mirror the actions.

1. Diagonal High Right to Low Left
2. Diagonal High Left to Low Right
3. Diagonal Low Right to High Left
4. Diagonal Low Left to High Right
5. Forehand Stab
6. Horizontal Cut Right to Left
7. Backhand Stab
8. Horizontal Cut Left to Right
9. Vertical Cut Down
10. Forward Stab

Beginning actions to focus on: When starting to work this drill, one should focus on movement fluidity and work on keeping the weapon in motion, smoothly transitioning from one action to the next. Keep your non-weapon hand 'active' at chest level and between you and the weapon hand. At this point, focus on the knife hand's movement and do not worry about what movement your non-weapon hand is doing. Later in the variations, we will explore non-weapon hand movements during these drills.

Starting with the basic actions of the drill to develop fluidity and target precision, the student will start from the first action of cutting diagonal high right to low left; at the end of that cut, the hand will roll up on the left side to cut diagonal high left to low right, and then roll back up on the right side for the first cut again. These two cuts can be done in succession repeatedly, making an infinity symbol in the air.

Next, this drill can be followed with a cut diagonal low right to high left, rolling down on the left side into cutting diagonal low left to high right, then rolling down the right side and starting over, as before.

Now we can combine all the diagonal cuts into one flowing drill. Start with the first action of cutting diagonal high right to low left, rolling up on the left side to cut diagonal high left to low right. From here, roll your knife and your hand over from pronation to supination, and start the next actions by cutting diagonal low right to high left, rolling down on the left side into cutting diagonal low left to high right. You have just completed all four of the diagonal cuts. To repeat, just roll your hand over as before and start your first action again.

As this drill is practiced and repeated, remember to breathe. I know that sounds crazy, but I have experienced many times that when performers are learning this drill, they tend to hold their breath during the movements. Focus on naturally breathing through the actions. Another element you can do is add a sound on the cut when it hits the center of the target. Any sound will work as long as it is supported by the breath.

It is time to incorporate the forehand and backhand stabs along with the horizontal cuts in with the diagonal cut drill. This is done after the last diagonal cut, diagonal low left to high right. After the cut, flow into a forehand stab to your partner's left side abdomen. Then immediately retract the action, roll your hand from pronation to supination (clockwise), and cut horizontally from right to left. After the cut, stab with a backhand thrust in supination, this time to your partner's right side. Again, immediately retract the action, and now roll your hand from supination to pronation (counterclockwise) and horizontal cut across from your left to right on the same line as the previous horizontal cut.

Now, to finish the drill, we will add the vertical cut down and the forward stab.

After finishing your left to right horizontal cut, roll your knife up and come into a downward vertical cut, then pull the blade back and stab center with a forward thrust with the hand in half-pronated (thumb up, palm facing inside). You can immediately retract the knife and return to on-guard or start the whole drill again.

Now that all the cuts and stabs have been incorporated into the drill, practice them all together in one flowing action. Again, remember to breathe through the action and keep your knife constantly in motion.

From the Ground Up

Let us now start exploring the physical relation between the body and the knife, using this drill as a tool for total body connection.

Getting the body into the action: First, we are going to stand in the basic on-guard stance. For now, just let your arms hang, relaxed, at your sides. Feel your connection to the floor through your feet and legs and remember to keep your knees slightly bent. Shift your body around slowly while focusing on your hips, keeping your feet in place and paying attention to the connection between your body and your feet. Feel how each body movement connects to your feet in either a push or pull action.

Now, try to focus on just moving your hips slowly by pushing your left hip forward, right hip back, and vice versa. Feel that connection all the way down your leg and how your feet are pushing or pulling on the ground. Also notice the reaction on your upper body as you push your hips back and forth. Notice how your shoulders are keeping their connection to your hips through your back and abdomen. To amplify this connection, allow whichever shoulder is moving forward to slightly dip into the action and the opposite shoulder to slightly rise away from the action. Try reversing it to where the shoulder slightly rises into the forward action and dips as it is moving away. Now let us look at adding in the previous drill.

We will begin with incorporating the shoulders and hips into the previous drill with the knife. For this, we will keep the feet in our basic on-guard stance.

Let the hips move with the shoulders during the cuts. For the first action, the diagonal high right to low left, your left hip will roll back and your right hip will roll forward; your right shoulder will roll down with the cut. Remember to let the initial energy start at your feet, working its way through your body and ending with the knife/hand being pulled through the target.

As you roll your right shoulder up, preparing for the next cut, let the right hip move back and the left hip roll forward as your right shoulder drops with the action of the diagonal high left to low right.

With the upward diagonal cuts, your hips are going to work the same way as the previous two cuts, but this time your shoulders are going to roll up with each cut.

Combine all the diagonal cuts together in a repeated pattern as before. Feel how your hips and shoulders are working as a conduit between your feet and the knife. Notice how on all attacks from your right, your right hip and shoulder are moving forward, and on your left your left hip and shoulder are pushing forward.

The forehand stab is going to be a quick forward and backward action with your hips and shoulders before your right hip and shoulder pushes the horizontal cut across from the right to the left side. The backhand stab will also have that quick back-and-forth push of your right hip and shoulder, followed by a forward push from your left hip as your right shoulder is pulled back for the horizontal cut from the left to the right.

For the vertical cut down and forward stab, we are going to have that same physical energy we had for the forehand stab, followed by the horizontal cut right to left. The right hip will push forward with the cut down and back on the recovery before pushing forward again on the forward stab. From the stab, you can reset into your basic on-guard stance.

To add even more dynamics to this drill, add a switch step between cuts, so that all cuts and thrusts from the right that you perform have the right foot forward, and all actions from the left have the left foot forward.

By this point, you should be fully engaged with your body in the actions of the knife. Having this connection from feet to knife make fights more engaging and dynamic. From this point on, always engage your whole body while working actions so that it becomes second nature when moving the knife that your body is connected to the action and telling a fully physical story.

Casting

To prevent bruising and sore arms in choreography, it is highly recommended that the performer of the actions executes each cut to the target while **casting** the energy forward and not into their partner. There are many names for the directing or redirecting of energy in stage combat, such as *reversal of tension, reverse energy, negative energy,* and *giving grace.* I have always used the term *casting* because most individuals I have worked with understood the use of a fishing rod, and the concept of sending the energy forward and past the tip of the weapon or hand was easier to understand. In stage combat, we never want to direct our full energy into someone. Even on contact hits, we control how much energy we put into our partner. Here in knife fighting, although our partner will be making contact during the block, there should never be so much energy in the action that the moves become out of control.

Casting Drill:

To practice casting your cuts, stand in front of your partner in distance. In a basic on-guard stance, "shoot" (quickly extend) your knife arm out, but do not hyperextend your elbow, to start the action of a diagonal high right to low left cut. However, in this drill, stop your weapon 2 to 3 inches away from your target of your partner's left shoulder.

The technique here is to send all your energy forward and not into your partner. Also try not to pull your energy back, as your arm will appear to 'bounce' off your target zone. When executed properly, your attack will look as if it has full energy and intention of hitting the target but comes to a sudden stop.

Continue doing this for each cut, paying attention to the energy you put into the action and the dissipation of that energy at the target.

Variation Drills

Active Hand Drills

These drills are designed to work your non-weapon hand in the previously described drill. Keep your non-weapon hand open and relaxed at chest level or whichever level the guard you are in requires.

High–Low: In this variation, the performer will move their non-weapon hand in a vertical motion up and down, opposite of where the knife hand is as it moves through the drill. Go slow and find the transitions; when the knife hand starts high, the other hand is low, and when the knife hand moves low, the other hand goes high.

Opposite sides: In this variation, the performer will move their non-weapon hand in a horizontal motion left and right, opposite of where the knife hand is as it moves through the drill. Go slow and find the transitions; when the knife hand starts right, the other hand is left, and when the knife hand moves left, the other hand goes right. This exercise is a great start to learning the 'scissoring' actions explored later in the book.

Big/Small Drill

This drill can be executed with either large actions or tight cuts.

For big actions, fully extend the attacking arm out and away from your targets and cut through them. This gives the look of someone who is cutting wild and is either untrained or in fear.

For small actions, keep everything close to the body. The cuts should not travel more than 6 inches before turning into the next action. This gives the impression of a highly skilled fighter.

Stab-Cut Drill

This drill is good for practicing back and forth actions between cuts and shows how any stab can turn into a cut.

Start with a forehand stab to your target's left shoulder, then rotate the knife clockwise and cut diagonal high right to low left. Retract the knife and stab with a backhand stab to the right hip area of your target, then retract the knife and stab with a backhand stab to your target's right shoulder, followed by rotating the knife counterclockwise and cut diagonal high left to low right.

Retract the knife and stab with a forehand stab to the left hip area of your target, retract and rotate clockwise into a diagonal low left to high right cut. Retract the knife and stab with a backhand stab to your target's right shoulder, repeating the actions of before; retract the knife and stab with a backhand stab to your target's right hip, followed by a retraction and rotation counterclockwise and cut diagonally low right to high left. Retract the knife and stab with a forehand stab to your target's left shoulder.

This time we are going to rotate the knife 'in' the target. Start with a forehand stab to your target's left abdomen, then rotate the knife clockwise and draw the cut across the abdomen from left to right before retracting the knife. Now perform a backhand stab to your target's right abdomen, rotate the knife counterclockwise, and cut horizontally across from right to left. Now target the sternum or upper chest with a forward stab, followed by drawing the cut down to the stomach/lower torso/groin area. Retract the knife and stab with a forward stab to the lower center torso.

Switching Grips

This drill will give the performer the experience of cutting and stabbing with underhand grips. These are almost exactly the same actions as the previous drill, but there are a few shifts in the actions. To start with, all clockwise and counterclockwise directions will be reversed. To add in the vertical upwards cut, we will change the last vertical down cut and turn it into a vertical cut up, starting in the stomach/lower torso/groin area and moving up to the upper chest. The final stab will be a downward stab to the chest.

Non-Dominant Hand

In this drill, you will start with the knife in the non-dominant hand and go through the cut diagram. This drill is great at building dexterity in both hands and facilitates double weapon work for more advanced knife fighting techniques and choreography. Pay attention to the body connection with the knife. I recommend shifting your stance to a left-foot-forward on-guard stance.

Switching Hands

In this drill, you will start with the knife in your dominant hand, then you will switch hands between each cut. Pay attention to how your body/hips/shoulders are all working together with each cut. Don't rush this exercise.

Example:

Right Hand Cut – Diagonal High to Low from the Right
Left Hand Cut – Diagonal High to Low from the Left
Right Hand Cut – Diagonal Low to High from the Right
Left Hand Cut – Diagonal Low to High from the Left
Right Hand Stab – Forehand Stab followed by a Horizontal Cut Right to Left
Left Hand Stab – Forehand Stab followed by a Horizontal Cut Left to Right
Right Hand Cut – Vertical Cut Down followed by a Forward Stab
Left Hand Cut – Vertical Cut Down followed by a Forward Stab

Swipes

Swipes are big actions that can add strong movements to choreography. They can be aimed anywhere on the body of your partner but are commonly aimed towards the head, belly, or feet of the performer. One of the biggest tricks to swipes is a large wind-up and leading the forward action with the pommel of the weapon (**Cue**), once the performer is clear of the action via a jump, duck, or avoidance (**Reaction**), allowing the blade to pass through the original target zone (**Action**).

As we start to explore some partnered exercises, it is important to take the time to talk about **Cue–Reaction–Action**, which is also known as *Action–Reaction–Action*, *Eye Contact–Preparation–Reaction–Action*, or *Preparation–Reaction–Action*. In this sequence, the performers work together in the process of giving and taking during the moves. The first **cue** is given by the attacker's initial action and starting point of the attack. The **reaction** is that of the victim who, taking the cue, gives the proper response, allowing for the final **action** between the two combatants to finish the move.

To start with, both partners should be out of distance in the beginning while learning these actions. Once the technique is understood and can be performed correctly multiple times, then the partners can enter into in-distance work, where the avoidance will take the performer away from a potential hit.

The Head Swipe

In this action, the attacker (**A**) performs a large action swipe at the defender's (**B**) head. The target area is just in line with **B**'s head while standing normally. When performed correctly in distance, this straight attack will look good.

Although **A** can hold the knife in almost any grip for this action, this drill is going to focus on an overhand saber grip.

A will start with an exaggerated wind-up preparatory action. This lets **B** know which attack is coming. For the head swipe, **A** wants to wind up on a high right or left line. For this drill, the performer should prep the action for the right to left head swipe.

A starts the swipe leading with the pommel of the weapon, and as the attack moves forward, **B** will react by squatting under the attack, bending at the knees and not the waist.

Once **B** squats, **A** can let the blade of the knife move forward and lead the swipe. **A**'s attack will pass above **B**'s head at the original target zone.

B will recover by standing.

Variation:

B can avoid back, lean back, or step back away from the attack.

The Belly/Stomach Swipe

In this action, the attacker (**A**) performs a large action swipe at the defender's (**B**) belly/stomach. The target area is **B**'s stomach while standing normally and performed in distance.

A starts with an exaggerated wind-up preparatory action. This lets **B** know which attack is coming. For the belly swipe, **A** wants to wind up on a middle line.

A starts the attack leading with the pommel of the weapon, and as the attack moves forward, **B** will lift their arms and, pushing their buttocks backward, will jump back away from the attack. The performers should be aware of distance, and **B** should keep their weapon away from *A*'s face when lifting and jumping back. Once **B** jumps, **A** can let the blade of the knife move forward and lead the swipe, as *A*'s attack passes through the original target zone of **B**'s stomach, after which **B** recovers to an on-guard stance.

The Legs/Feet Swipe

In this action, the attacker (**A**), from a kneeling position, performs a large action swipe at the defender's (**B**) legs/feet. The target area is **B**'s lower shins/feet while standing normally and performed in distance.

A starts with an exaggerated wind-up preparatory action. This lets **B** know which attack is coming. For the shins/feet swipe, *A* will be kneeling and will wind up on a low middle line.

A starts the attack leading with the pommel of the weapon, and as the attack moves forward, **B** will lift their knees while jumping up in the air, vertically away from the attack; **B** could also jump backward. The performers should be aware of distance, and **B** should keep their weapon away from *A*'s face when jumping. Once **B** jumps, **A** can let the blade of the knife move forward and lead the swipe, as *A*'s attack passes through the original target zone of **B**'s lower legs, after which **B** recovers to an on-guard stance and *A* recovers to a standing position or preps for another attack.

Variation:

B can be in an exaggerated stance with one leg farther forward. *A* can target just that one leg on the attack, at which point **B** can just lift the leg up and either replace it back down or in the lift step away from the action.

Diagonal Swipes

Diagonal swipes are just exaggerated high to low, or low to high, cuts on the diagonal. In this technique, *A* will attack with an exaggerated high right to low left cut. This is exaggerated by being larger than the normal diagonal cut you usually perform, by extending the arm and putting your full body into the action and cutting from above the head all the way through the target zone. Here, **B** will avoid the attack by displacing out with their left foot and leaning their body towards the step. Remember to keep your knife and hand active during the avoidance. The body of **B** and the cut of **A** should be at the same diagonal. After the cut, **B** should recover back to on-guard. This can be done in the opposite direction, and it can also be done with rising cuts as opposed to descending cuts.

Closing Comments

In this chapter, we explored some of the basic offensive actions of the knife. We learned new terminology that will help us better understand the actions we are doing and will give us a good foundation as we move forward. The concepts of distance, targets, flow, and casting were introduced and explored, and will be continued in later chapters of this book.

Understanding characterization and what style they would use is important in telling the story, and that is what the job is — telling a story. Flow and body dynamics can make or break choreography. If a character is not skilled in knife fighting, having them look like they have spent years training will break the dramatic convention. The same goes in the opposite direction; if the character is a trained killer but they are timid, off-balance, overly exaggerating their actions, or just not connected to the fight, all characterization goes right out the window. This is why we will continue to work on flow and body dynamics in each chapter, building on the principles learned in the previous chapter.

We are now starting to combine all the actions, grips, guards, and theories from previous chapters, and will do so even more as we progress through the book. I highly recommend having a strong understanding of this chapter before moving on, as everything up to this point will be needed and used in the training moving forward.

6

BLOCKS, DEFLECTIONS, AND CHECKS

Now we are going to introduce and explore blocks, checks, and transporting actions. It is in these actions where I find that knife fighting really gets interesting and strategic. Suddenly, basic actions become a game of chess between combatants where the drama and tension can be built and the structure of the story can take place. In this chapter, we will explore the concepts of armed and unarmed defensive actions. We will also look at the many ways performers and directors can change up the basic elements of a fight to create truly dynamic choreography, one in which all the actions carry the story forward.

Safety Notes

In this chapter and those that follow, we will be discussing two performers at the same time, as we will need an attacker and a defender. There are many issues that arise when working in pairs, and we will address these

DOI: 10.4324/9781003147862-6

issues in each section. The main safety point to remember when working with a partner is to be slow and respectful while learning these actions. Some people are better at picking up new concepts or have better physical awareness than others. Remember that you are partners working on a scene, not adversaries in a real fight. For these exercises, partners will need to be in-distance and close enough that forearms can make contact without having to overextend or lean into the actions. I also highly recommend, as performers are starting to learn these actions for the first time, that neither of the performers are holding anything. All these actions can be done unarmed by simply going through the actions with empty hands. As the performers increase their skills, training weapons can be added, and once the techniques are fully understood and able to be performed without mistakes, only then should the performers begin to use their theatrical weapons.

Chapter notes: This section presents all actions for a right-handed performer; left-handed performers can mirror the actions. In each of the exercises in the next section, as in the previous chapter, the attacker will always be referred to as **A**, while the defender of the initial action will always be referred to as **B**.

Blocks

For many performers and directors, the terms to block or blocking generally brings up the notion of moving and positioning performers on the stage. However, in theatrical combat, blocks are actions used to stop or deflect an oncoming attack and can be performed on either side of the body and in all lines.

When dealing with blocks, there are four basic ways in which these actions can be performed:

Opposition: This is where the defending hand or arm is brought up as a barrier or shield, and fully stops the action and energy of the attack.

Displace: This is where the defending hand or arm manipulates the attack and deflects or redirects the energy of the action away from its intended target.

Beat: This is where the defending hand or arm deflects the attack by "beating" it away from its intended target.

Offensive: This is where the defending hand or arm strikes into the attack with the intention to strike and incapacitate rather than block or displace.

Opposition Blocks (also known as Static Blocks)

As we begin our understanding of the defensive actions of knife work, I have found that it is best to start with the simple defensive **static blocks** in relation to the ten-cut system from the previous chapter. These static blocks are intended to fully stop the action and energy of the attacker's actions and develop the basic concepts of blocks for the performer, on which we will build for more advanced actions later in the chapter.

To prevent bruising and sore arms, it is highly recommended that in these exercises, the performer of the actions executes each cut to the target while casting the energy forward and not into their partner.

It is also important to note that while blocking, it is helpful to use the muscle mass on the back (same side as backhand) of the forearm as opposed to the foreside (little finger edge) of the arm, where the ulna bone is less protected. When blocking an attack, it is best to target the middle of your forearm to the middle of your partner's forearm. There will be times when you will use your hands, or target a different part of your partner's arm, and those actions will be explained later in the chapter. For now, focus on using the middle section of the back of your forearm to make connection with the middle of the attacker's inner forearm.

Tips and Tricks to Remember While You Learn

Eye contact: As you learn these techniques, maintain eye contact with your partner and be in the moment. Do not try to watch the hands or weapons. There will be moments in choreography where you may want the character to watch the weapons, such as if you want them to look terrified and unskilled, but otherwise try to focus on maintaining eye contact with your partner.

For beginning performers, it is always a good idea to have the attacks exaggerated and moving slowly. Speed is the enemy of good fight choreography; remember, we want the audience (and our partner) to see the action. Speed is also the enemy of learning proper technique. As the saying goes, "Slow is smooth, smooth is fast".

As *A* attacks, the energy of the attack should stop before reaching **B**'s body; this casting of energy prevents performers from bruising or injuring each other during the exercises.

Work on timing. As **B** blocks, their arm should meet *A*'s arm. *A* should be casting their energy past **B** and not into them. Try to avoid slamming or hitting arms together. Even with using the back of the forearm, this can cause bruising and fatigue of the arms. When done properly, it will look as if the arms are meeting with force (acted percussion), but they actually will meet at the right point of contact where excessive energy is not being placed into either of the performer's arms. A fight will always look fake if either the attack or the block is just holding in the air before the other joins or connects. The goal of this is to have each arm meet at the end of the action together.

Always remember to keep the non-blocking hand active and in a ready position.

When turning the hand, always turn it on the inside line. When cross blocking on the high line and turning your hand to be palm in, always think of bringing your little finger in towards you, not turning it away from you. When cross blocking on the low lines, do the opposite and turn your thumb in and pinky out, so that the back of your forearm is always making contact with your partner.

Combining any block with footwork or pivoting makes the fight choreography more dramatic, dynamic, and believable.

Pivots can be done with footwork or torso twists. The performers can utilize footwork described in previous chapters or allow the torso to twist. Be careful of twisting too much and causing pulled muscles in the back. Your spine should always be in alignment and supported with your skeleton.

Single-Arm Static Blocks

Here we will perform the basic static blocks with the non-weapon-bearing arm.

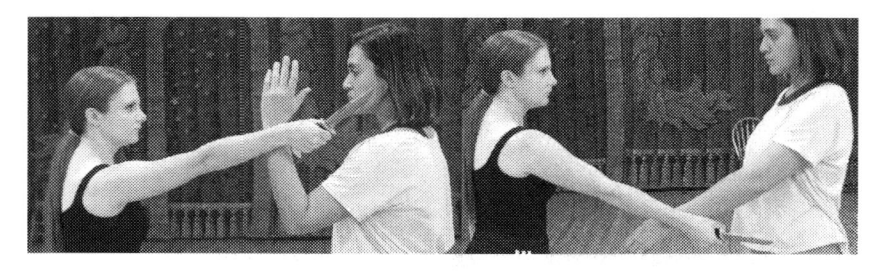

Figure 6.1 Single-Arm Static Block

1. As the attacker (**A**) starts the actions with the first cut to the left shoulder of the blocker (**B**), **B** can then extend the left arm forward, elbow bent at 90 degrees, and make connection with **A**'s forearm with the back of their forearm (see Figure 6.1).
2. As **A** cuts to the right shoulder, **B** pivots to the right and extends the left arm forward, elbow bent at 90 degrees, making connection with **A**'s forearm with the back of their forearm by rotating the palm of the hand inside.
3. As **A** cuts to the left hip, **B** extends the left arm forward and low, making connection with **A**'s forearm with the back of their forearm (see Figure 6.1).
4. As **A** cuts to the right hip, **B** pivots right and extends the left arm forward and low, making connection with **A**'s forearm with the back of their forearm.
5. As **A** stabs/thrusts in a pronated action to the left side, **B** extends the left arm low and forward, elbow bent at 90 degrees, making connection with **A**'s forearm with the back of their forearm.
6. As **A** cuts from **B**'s left to right on the midline, **B** extends the left arm low and forward, elbow bent at 90 degrees, making connection with **A**'s forearm with the back of their forearm.
7. As **A** stabs/thrusts in a supinated action to the right side, **B** pivots right and extends the left arm low and forward, elbow bent at 90 degrees, making connection with **A**'s forearm with the back of their forearm.

8. As **A** cuts from **B**'s right to left on the midline, **B** pivots right and extends the left arm low and forward, elbow bent at 90 degrees, making connection with **A**'s forearm with the back of their forearm.
9. As **A** cuts down, **B** extends the left arm up, elbow bent at 90 degrees, above the head, palm facing down, making connection with **A**'s forearm with the back of their forearm.
10. As **A** attacks with a forward stab action to center line, **B** extends the left arm low and forward along the center line and making connection with **A**'s forearm with the back of their forearm, as **B** sidesteps with a pivot towards the right, or sidesteps with a pivot left if cross blocking with the left arm.

Double-Arm Static Blocks

Double-arm static blocks can be used with or without a weapon. These blocks are good choices if we want to show that one character is stronger than the other, or if we want to set up for a counter action. These blocks usually require the defensive side to step into the action, or at least turn into the incoming attack. This block is not recommended for all actions of attack; however, we will examine most of the cuts and the double block response. A note of safety here is to make sure the blocks stay on the forearm of the attacker and not the elbow or wrist (see Figure 6.2).

Figure 6.2 Double-Arm Static Block

1. As the attacker (**A**) starts the actions with the first cut to the left shoulder of the blocker (**B**), **B** pivots to their left and, using both forearms, blocks the incoming attack. Both elbows are bent at 90 degrees and making connection with **A**'s forearm with the back of their forearms. In this block, **B**'s right arm will be closest to **A**'s body, and the left arm will be closest to **A**'s wrist.

2. As **A** cuts to the right shoulder, **B** pivots to their right and extends their arms forward, elbows bent at 90 degrees, making connection with **A**'s forearm with the back of their forearms. In this block, **B**'s left arm will be closest to **A**'s body, and the right arm will be closest to **A**'s wrist.

3. As **A** cuts to the left hip, **B** pivots to the left and extends their arms forward and low, making connection with **A**'s forearm with the back of their forearms. In this block, **B**'s right arm will be closest to **A**'s body, and the left arm will be closest to **A**'s wrist.

4. As **A** cuts to the right hip, **B** pivots to the right and extends their arm forward and low, making connection with **A**'s forearm with the back of their forearms. In this block, **B**'s left arm will be closest to **A**'s body, and the right arm will be closest to **A**'s wrist.

5. As **A** stabs/thrusts in a pronated action to the left side, **B** pivots to their left and extends the left arm low and forward and the right arm low and forward with the elbow bent at 90 degrees. **B** makes connection with **A**'s forearm with the back of their forearms, with the right hand above and left hand below the attacking arm. In this block, **B**'s right arm will be closest to **A**'s body, and the left arm will be closest to **A**'s wrist.

6. As **A** cuts from **B**'s left to right on the midline, **B** pivots to their left and extends the left arm low and forward and the right arm low and forward with the elbow bent at 90 degrees. **B** makes connection with **A**'s forearm with the back of their forearms, with the right hand above and left hand below the attacking arm. In this block, **B**'s right arm will be closest to **A**'s body, and the left arm will be closest to **A**'s wrist.

7. As **A** stabs/thrusts in a supinated action to the right side, **B** pivots to their right and extends the right arm low and forward and the left arm low and forward with the elbow bent at 90 degrees. **B** makes connection with **A**'s forearm with the back of their forearms, with the left hand above and right hand below the attacking arm. In this block, **B**'s left arm will be closest to **A**'s body, and the right arm will be closest to **A**'s wrist.

8. As **A** cuts from **B**'s right to left on the midline, **B** pivots to their right and extends the right arm low and forward and the left arm low and forward with the elbow bent at 90 degrees. **B** makes connection with **A**'s forearm with the back of their forearms, with the left hand above and right hand below the attacking arm. In this block, **B**'s left arm will be closest to **A**'s body, and the right arm will be closest to **A**'s wrist.

9. As **A** cuts down, **B** extends both their right and left arms up, elbows bent at 90 degrees, above the head, palms facing down, making connection with **A**'s forearm with the back of their forearms. In this position, both of **B**'s arms are bent towards each other, forearms side by side, with the back of both forearms towards **A**'s attack.

X-Blocks

The X-block is where both arms are crossed, usually below the elbow at mid-forearm, while catching the attacking arm or leg in the open "V" between the hands. X-blocks can be used with or without a weapon and in all lines of attack. These blocks can be a more dynamic choice if we want to show that one character is stronger than the other, and a great choice should we want to set up for a counter action. These blocks usually require the defensive side to step into the action, or at least turn into the incoming attack. Although X-blocks are effective blocks, they are most effective when followed immediately by a secondary action. An X-block on its own without a follow-up action can make a fight look static and break the flow of action in storytelling (see Figure 6.3).

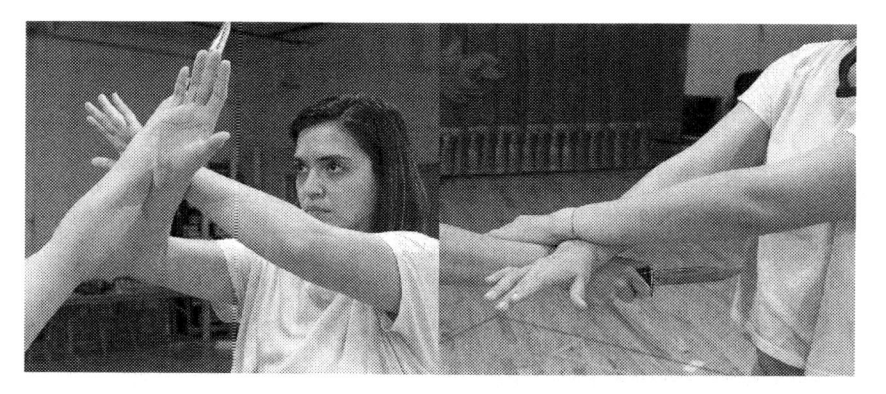

Figure 6.3 X-Block

1. As the attacker (**A**) starts the actions with the first cut to the left shoulder of the blocker (**B**), **B** pivots to their left and, using both upper forearms, blocks the incoming attack. In this block, **B**'s right arm will be closest to **A**'s body, and the left arm will be closest to **A**'s wrist.
2. As **A** cuts to the right shoulder, **B** pivots to their right and blocks the incoming attack. In this block, **B**'s left arm will be closest to **A**'s body, and the right arm will be closest to **A**'s wrist.
3. As **A** cuts to the left hip, **B** pivots to the left and extends their arms forward and low. In this block, **B**'s right arm will be closest to **A**'s body, and the left arm will be closest to **A**'s wrist.
4. As **A** cuts to the right hip, **B** pivots to the right and extends their arm forward and low. In this block, **B**'s left arm will be closest to **A**'s body, and the right arm will be closest to **A**'s wrist.
5. As **A** stabs/thrusts in a pronated action to the left side, **B** pivots to their left and blocks the incoming attack. In this block, **B**'s right arm will be closest to **A**'s body, and the left arm will be closest to **A**'s wrist.
6. As **A** cuts from **B**'s left to right on the midline, **B** pivots to their left and blocks the incoming attack. In this block, **B**'s right arm will be closest to **A**'s body, and the left arm will be closest to **A**'s wrist.
7. As **A** stabs/thrusts in a supinated action to the right side, **B** pivots to their right and blocks the incoming attack. In this block, **B**'s left arm

will be closest to **A**'s body, and the right arm will be closest to **A**'s wrist.

8. As **A** cuts from **B**'s right to left on the midline, **B** pivots to their right and blocks the incoming attack. In this block, **B**'s left arm will be closest to **A**'s body, and the right arm will be closest to **A**'s wrist.

9. As **A** cuts down, **B** extends both their right and left arms up, above the head, making connection with **A**'s forearm with the back of their forearm. Either arm can be forward in this block.

10. As **A** attacks with a forward stab action to center line, **B** extends both their right and left arms forward and low, below the chest, palms facing down, making connection with **A**'s forearm. Either arm can be forward in this block.

Note: Although most of the time we want to catch the attack in the open "V" created between the hands, there can be situations where the open "V" between a hand and an elbow can be utilized, depending on character and choreography. However, there is very rarely an option for catching an action in the "V" between the elbows.

Active Blocks

Unlike static blocks, which completely stop the action of the attack, active blocks are in-motion defensive actions that can displace, beat, or be offensive actions, such as stabbing the attacking arm. As we explore active blocks, we are going to start with passthrough actions against the attack. After passthroughs, we will explore additional actions that can be done with or after the initial block, such as checking, replacements, transfers, and expulsions. In these sections, we will also explore the use of hands in blocking and directing actions and look at other areas on the attacking arm which can be targeted by the defender.

To help prevent any injuries, it is highly recommended that in this exercise, the performer of the offensive actions executes each cut with a flow-through action, where the knife continues its cut through the target zone, while performers are out of distance with each other and start with empty hands before moving to training knives. Only once the moves are well understood and both performers have good control, can the performers then close distance.

Passthrough Actions on Cuts

Performers should be starting out of distance, and with this exercise the attacker's actions are not stopped but instead are pushed through by the defender. The defender should not attempt to grab hold of the attacker's arm; instead, they should focus on just pushing it through the action by getting behind the forearm with their open hand and following its natural movement. Grabs will be covered in the next chapter.

Things to Pay Attention to

Watch out for slapping actions. These actions should be pushes, and the defender should not be making strong contact with the attacker's arm.

Cup (keeping your thumb pressed against the side of your hand) your unarmed defensive hand instead of trying to grab your partner's arm. Creating a nice hook hand will be safer and more useful in choreography than trying to open the thumb and grab the arm. This will be covered more in the next chapter.

The first two diagonal down cuts:

1. As the attacker (**A**) starts the actions with the first cut to the left shoulder of the blocker (**B**), **B** can extend the left arm forward, making connection with the back of **A**'s forearm with their hand from under the attack. The attack is then pushed down and through the action as **B,** who is already out of distance, leans away from the attack.

2. As **A** cuts to the right shoulder, **B** extends the left arm forward, making connection with the back of **A**'s forearm with their hand from above the attack and making sure to keep the left elbow out of the line of attack. The attack is then pushed down and through the action as **B**, who is already out of distance, leans away from the attack.

The two diagonal up cuts:

3. As **A** cuts to the left hip, **B** extends the left arm forward and low, making connection with the back of **A**'s forearm with their hand

from above the attack. The attack is then pushed up and through the action as **B**, who is already out of distance, leans away from the attack.

4. As **A** cuts to the right hip, **B** extends the left arm forward and low, making connection with the back of **A**'s forearm with their hand from above the attack. The attack is then pushed up and through the action as **B**, who is already out of distance, leans away from the attack.

The two horizontal cuts:

5. As **A** cuts from **B**'s left to right on the midline, **B** extends the left arm forward, making connection with the back of **A**'s forearm with their hand from above the attack. The attack is then pushed through the action to **B**'s right as **B**, who is already out of distance, leans away from the attack.

6. As **A** cuts from **B**'s right to left on the midline, **B** extends the left arm forward, making connection with the back of **A**'s forearm with their hand from above the attack. The attack is then pushed through the action to **B**'s left as **B**, who is already out of distance, leans away from the attack.

The vertical cuts:

7. As **A** cuts down, **B** extends the left arm up, making connection with the back of **A**'s forearm with their hand. The attack is then pushed down through the action as **B**, who is already out of distance, leans away from the attack.

8. As **A** cuts up, **B** extends the left arm down, making connection with the back of **A**'s forearm with their hand. The attack is then pushed up through the action as **B**, who is already out of distance, leans away from the attack.

Closing the Distance:
Once the previously described techniques have been learned and are repeatable by both performers, distance should now be closed. Once in-distance, the defender should step away from the attack, providing space

for the action to pass through, then immediately step back into distance if responding with an attack.

Secondary Actions After the Block

Checking Actions

To make a fight more dynamic, **checking** actions can be added into the fight. A check is the process of curbing or restraining the offending hand or arm after a successful block. The defending hand or arm remains in contact with the opponent's (without gripping, locking, or holding) in order to sense their movements, feel or control the placement of the offending limb, and use that to both offensive and defensive advantage. These actions control the opposing hand or arm and may maintain it or remove it with the action of an expulsion or transport.

Replacement Blocks

Replacement blocks are blocks that use both hands/arms, one after the other, to deflect and control the offending hand or arm. One hand begins the block; the other is then used to complete the block, checking the offending limb and freeing the first hand for a counterattack. It is important to remember in choreography that we are working together to tell the story. It is all too easy for either the attacker or defender to present an action with unnecessary excessive force. Again, we want to make sure we are meeting each other, and not slamming or banging arms together.

With this technique, the attack will be blocked by the hand holding the knife in either a static same-side or cross-body block. Once the block is successful, the opposite arm − in this case, the left arm − will replace the block, allowing the right arm to return to ready position. It is important for beginning students to go slow and allow extra time for the action by allowing the attacking arm to hang in the air as the defender learns the technique of replacement blocks. Once the performer gains control and skill in this technique, not only will the replacement block be a smooth continuous action but a counter action also can be added, instead of returning to ready position.

Example of the action:

> The attack starts with a cut to the left shoulder of the blocker (**B**). **B** can then do a small pivot to the left, extend the right arm forward, and make the connection with **A**'s forearm. Once the block is made, the left arm can reach out and be placed against the attacker's forearm, between the original block and the attacker's wrist. **B** can then withdraw the right arm to a ready position while pivoting back to center, aligned with **A**'s center line.

> Personal note of preference: Although there are good reasons in choreography to do a replacement block on the arm to attacks coming to the defender's right side – such as counters, locks, throws, or disarms – I personally will usually opt for a quicker and more direct action. For an attack coming to the right side of the defender, I prefer checking the arm up on the bicep area with an open hand after blocking with the right arm. The main reason for this technique is that it is a closer target of opportunity for the left hand, and I do not have to reach across my body to control the attacker. Something to pay attention to is to not be on the elbow or shoulder but instead centered on the upper arm.

Transports

A transport is a checking action made on the opponent's hand or arm and executed by blocking the attack and then moving it vertically from a high line to a low line, or from a low line to a high line on the same side as where the block took place. These actions allow the defender to open lines of attack after successfully making a block. Using transports, or any form of check actions, during a fight create a more dynamic and active choreography.

Transports can be performed after any successful block. In this exercise, we are going to combine it with the replacement block we learned previously. The trick to making a transport look natural is to execute the action at the same time as the withdrawal of the defender's blocking arm. If one is doing a transport from a static block that does not include a replacement, then the transport should happen once the block is successful. Beginning performers tend to keep the pause in the performance that they learned in the practice of the technique. As the performer becomes more confident in their skill and ability, the transport should be executed immediately upon acquiring the block, without such a pause.

An example of this is as the attacker (**A**) starts the actions with the first cut to the left shoulder of the blocker (**B**), **B** can then do a small pivot to the left and extend the right arm forward, making connection with **A**'s forearm with the back of their forearm by rotating the palm of the hand inside. Once the block is made, the left arm can reach out at a high forward and place against the attacker's forearm, between the original block and the attacker's wrist. **B** can then withdraw the right arm to a ready position, while directing **A**'s attacking arm down towards **B**'s left hip. **B** pivots back to center with this action, aligning themself with **A**'s center line.

Tips and Tricks:

Always keep a relaxed, open hand when transporting your partner's arm; never grab their arm with force. We will go into grabs in the next chapter.

Always manipulate the attacker's arm towards the attacker and away from the defender's body when crossing, so that the weapon cannot make contact with the defender as it passes between the performers.

Always have control of your knife during an expulsion or transport; the energy of the move may cause the knife to slip out of the hand if not held properly.

Bind

A bind is a checking action made on the opponent's hand or arm and executed by blocking the attack and then moving it diagonally to the opposite quadrant (i.e., from the inside high to the outside low, or outside high to inside low, etc.).

An example of this is as the attacker (**A**) starts the actions with the first cut to the left shoulder of the blocker (**B**), **B** can do a small pivot to the left and extend the right arm forward, elbow bent at 90 degrees, making connection with **A**'s forearm with the back of their forearm by rotating the palm of the hand inside. Once the block is made, the left arm can reach out at a high forward with the elbow bent at 90 degrees and place against the attacker's forearm, between the original block and the attacker's wrist. **B** can then withdraw the right arm to a ready position while circling the left arm counterclockwise, manipulating **A**'s attacking arm down past **B**'s right hip. **B** pivots back to center with this action, aligning themself with **A**'s center line. **B** should make sure that they either push **A**'s arm closer to **A**'s body during the bind or slightly step back away from the action to prevent **A**'s knife from making contact with **B**.

Envelopment

An envelopment is a checking action made on the opponent's hand or arm, executed by blocking the attack and then by describing a circle with both arms in contact, bringing the opponent's arm back to the placement where the check began.

In this exercise, we are going to go back to the single left-arm static block on the attack, although like before, these techniques will work if you block with your knife arm and do a replacement block.

An example of this is as the attacker (**A**) starts the actions with the first cut to the left shoulder of the blocker (**B**), **B** can extend the left arm forward, elbow bent at 90 degrees, making connection with **A**'s forearm with the back of their forearm. **B** will then manipulate **A**'s arm in a counterclockwise circle down and around, back to the original position. As with the bind, **B** should make sure that they either push **A**'s arm closer to **A**'s body during the bind or slightly step back away from the action to prevent **A**'s knife from making contact with **B**.

Expulsions

As we come to an end of examining the variations of blocks, we now turn to a final action that can be added to any movement of the block or transport – the expulsion. An expulsion uses the energy and movement of a check to throw or fling the opposing arm aside. This simple action can add a level of energy and movement to a fight and show the skill of the fighters. Expulsions are performed by either redirecting the energy away during a static block or continuing the action of the transport, bind, or envelopment in an outward action of the attacker's arm, away from the body. While it is the defender that initiates the action of the expulsion, it is the attacker who controls the action.

Expulsions should feel a bit familiar to you, as you were starting to use them when you learned the passthrough blocks earlier in this chapter.

Next we will look at performing an expulsion on each of the blocks previously covered. Although we will only be using one example, know that an expulsion can be added to almost any block.

Static Blocks:

As the attacker (**A**) starts the actions with the first cut to the left shoulder of the blocker (**B**), **B** can extend the left arm forward, making connection with A's forearm with the back of their forearm. **B** then slides their open hand down to the forearm of **A** and pushes the arm away to **B**'s high left.

Cross-Body Static Blocks:

As the attacker (**A**) starts the actions with the first cut to the left shoulder of the blocker (**B**), **B** can do a small pivot to the left and extend the right arm forward, elbow bent at 90 degrees, making connection with **A**'s forearm with the back of their forearm by rotating the palm of the hand inside. **B** then slides their open hand down to the forearm of **A** and pushes **A**'s arm away while pivoting back to center, aligned with **A**'s center line. If **B**'s hand is holding the knife, then the back of the hand can be used.

Double-Arm Static Blocks:

As **A** cuts to the right shoulder, **B** pivots to their right and extends their arms forward, elbows bent at 90 degrees, making connection with **A**'s forearm with the back of their forearms. In this block, **B**'s left arm will be closest to **A**'s body, and the right arm will be closest to **A**'s wrist. **B** then slides their unarmed hand down to the forearm of **A** and pushes **A**'s arm away, while pivoting back to center, aligned with **A**'s center line.

X-Blocks:

As the attacker (**A**) starts the actions with the first cut to the left shoulder of the blocker (**B**), **B** pivots to their left and blocks the incoming attack. In this block, **B**'s right arm will be closest to **A**'s body, and the left arm will be closest to **A**'s wrist. **B** then uses their left (unarmed) hand and pushes **A**'s arm away to **B**'s high left while pivoting back to center, aligned with **A**'s center line.

Replacement Blocks:

As **A** cuts to the right shoulder, **B** blocks with the right arm. Once the block is made, the left arm can reach out at a high forward right against the attacker's forearm. Then as **B** withdraws the right arm to a ready position, **B** pushes **A**'s arm away to **B**'s high right.

Transports and Binds:

With transports and binds, continue the energy of the action out and away from the body, allowing **B**'s hand to slide down to **A**'s forearm with the action, then releasing that energy at the end.

Envelopments:

Envelopments are a combination of the transport/bind action finished with an expulsion action. **B** envelops **A**'s attack in a circular motion, allowing **B**'s hand to slide down to **A**'s forearm with the action. Once **A**'s arm returns to the original position, **B** pushes **A**'s arm away from their body.

Closing Comments

In this chapter, we started exploring the elements that help bring a knife fight together for the stage and screen. Actors should remember to start slow and allow each other to build the knowledge and skills needed to execute these moves, practicing good partnering skills. Once understood, performers can then bring the fight up to performance speed. There are almost endless ways to combine cuts, blocks, checks, and expulsions into a fight. Each performer, each style, and each choreography will have its own flow, and that is where the joy and beauty of a knife fight can come from. Although each performer is unique and different in how they move, they can help achieve the vision for the fight that best fits by listening to the choreographer and the director for what the scene calls for in that moment. Directors can help the fight choreographer and the performers by understanding exactly what the fight needs to convey, the emotional elements from each performer, and how the fight fits into the overall story at this moment in the show.

7

GRABS, LOCKS, AND DISARMS

In this chapter, we will explore the elements of grabs, locks, and disarms, both armed and unarmed techniques. I would like to clarify again that these techniques are for theatrical purposes only. They are not meant to be used in real situations. The actions here are only to be used between two performers who are working together to tell a story through physical action. There should never be any force applied to yourself or your partner that may cause harm in any way. When we are working with grabs and locks, the performers are always in full control of the actions. They are not trying to actually cause physical discomfort or injury. If you have been reading this book chapter by chapter, I know this sounds like a broken record. However, for those who are just jumping to sections they are wanting more information on, or advanced techniques, I feel it is always important to reiterate: SAFETY FIRST.

DOI: 10.4324/9781003147862-7

As in each of the previous chapters, we will start with the basic techniques and progress to the advanced actions. Always practice the techniques slowly until you have mastered the actions, before progressing to performance speed. In knife fighting, the reality is fast, sloppy, and close; in theatre, we want to open the space more and slow it down so both the performers and the audience can see what is happening and so that the choreography can be repeated consistently. Well-trained performers working with an experienced, qualified fight director can make a safe and repeatable fight look dangerous and realistic without ever compromising on safety or story.

Grabs

If you have studied unarmed stage combat before, you know that grabs are some of the most basic actions we do on stage. However, it seems to be the one action where performers always forget their training and go back to actually grabbing someone with force, which can result in bruising or injury during moments of staged violence. Adding a weapon to this mix can be even more dangerous. With this in mind, we will revisit the basics of grabs before moving on.

The purpose of this action is to create the illusion that the aggressor (**A**) is trying to manipulate their partner (**B**) by physically grabbing hold of their arm and moving them by force, by either a pulling or pushing action. This action can also be used as a restraining action from **A** in order to keep **B** from moving, in which case it should look like **A** is holding on to **B** with force, while **B** tries to pull or move away from the grip or lock. Body language is very important in selling the grab effectively.

Hand Positions for Grips

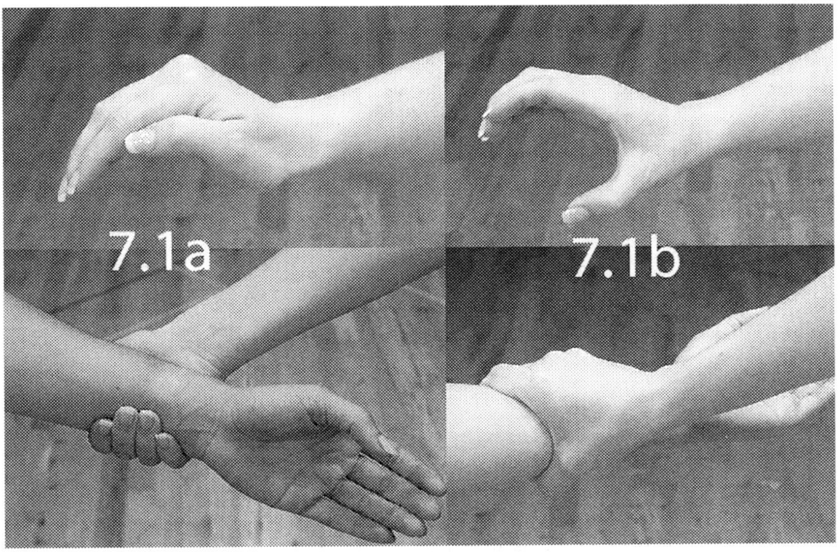

Figure 7.1 Hand Positions for Grips

There are two basic hand positions used for grasping on to someone. The first is the "hook" hand position, also known as a "cup" hand. Here the aggressor creates a hook with their hand, fingers together and curved with the thumb flat against the side of the hand (see Figure 7.1a).

The other is the "C" grip, also known as the clamp grip, claw grip, or toy hand grip. This is where the aggressor creates a "C" with their hand, fingers together and thumb open out – basically the same as the hook hand but with the thumb extended after contact is made (see Figure 7.1b).

In both positions, it is important to keep the fingers close together. This wide, flat surface allows for a solid contact area for both partners to work with, without small pressure areas that can easily cause bruising by turning the top of the fingertips into the partner's arm.

With these grips, we want to create the illusion that the aggressor is using force to restrain their partner. To do this, **A** must put tension in their hand and not put pressure on their partner. With a tense but open hand, **B** can pull or push against it without any discomfort to themselves.

As every move in a fight or struggle is choreographed, each partner knows exactly what is happening and when.

Locks

Locks are moves that immobilize parts of the body by applying pressure to the joints. With knife fighting, locks are great moves to use before or while disarming an opponent. We will examine three types of locks: wrist locks, arm bars, and shoulder locks. In each of these actions, the performer acting the pain is always in full control of their body, while the performer executing the lock follows their partner's cues and maintains light contact.

In theatrical combat, we NEVER perform any move that actually applies pressure to the joints. Instead, partners work together to create the illusion of pain while maintaining safe body postures to prevent any kind of injury or stress to their joints. As always, while learning new techniques, students should start slowly and pay attention to each other's cues and reactions.

Wrist lock

A wrist lock is a joint lock primarily affecting the wrist joint and is normally employed by grasping the person's hand and twisting and/or bending it. While there are four types of wrist locks – rotational (rotation of the wrist joint), hyperflexing (pushing the palm of the hand towards the forearm), hyperextending (pushing the back of the hand towards the forearm), and adductive (a forced ulnar deviation of the hand) – we are only going to work with rotational wrist locks against the knife-bearing hand of the attacker.

Rotational Wrist Locks

In practical tactical use, a rotational wrist lock involves forced twisting of the hand into a *pronated* or *supinated* position. The force of this twisting is transferred to the forearm, causing radioulnar rotation, as the joint of the wrist does not allow for rotating motions, eventually resulting in a lock on the radioulnar joint. Further twisting will put serious stress on the wrist joint. We do not want this in theatrical fighting; what we want is to give the illusion of this technique in a safe, repeatable way.

Pronated Wrist Lock

In this lock, the actor having their wrist locked by their partner will turn their right wrist counterclockwise (clockwise for left wrist), also known as 'internally rotating' the wrist. In this action, the elbow will turn away from the body. It should be noted that a bent elbow reduces rotation of the humerus. Therefore, straightening the arm allows rotation of the arm and lessens the pressure on the joints.

As the attacker (**A**) thrusts to center with the knife in their right hand, the unarmed defender (**B**) blocks the incoming attack with a left static block followed by a grab to **A**'s wrist with the right hand. **A** will then initiate the movement of the lock by rotating their hand counterclockwise. Once the right hand has turned, **A** will pivot to the left, leading with the right shoulder. **B** will follow **A**'s lead and allow a small pivot to the right, while placing the open left hand on **A**'s forearm. **B** can then perform a simple takeaway disarm (covered later in the chapter).

It is important to note here that **B** does not add any energy to **A**'s movement – they must simply follow the action. **B** should also be accurate with the placement of the left hand on the forearm only and avoid the elbow and shoulder, as these placements could add extra pressure to their partner's arm.

Supinated Wrist Lock

The supinated wrist lock is perhaps the most popular wrist lock, and it is similar to the pronated wrist lock except reversed in direction. The actor will rotate the hand clockwise (counterclockwise for left), also known as 'externally rotating' the wrist. In this action, the elbow will be turned into the body. Straightening the arm does not lessen the pressure.

As the attacker (**A**) thrusts to center with the knife in their right hand, the unarmed defender (**B**) blocks the incoming attack with a right static block followed by a grab to **A**'s wrist with the left hand. **A** will then initiate the movement of the lock by rotating their hand clockwise. Once the right hand has turned, **A** will pivot to the left slightly, tucking their right elbow into the body and lifting their sternum. **B** will follow **A**'s lead and allow a small pivot to the left. **B** can then do a right-forearm push to disarm the attacker (covered later in the chapter).

Arm Bar

A lock that hyperextends the elbow joint is referred to as an arm bar. In unarmed combat, there are several different types of arm bars/arm locks; some are designed for submissions, some for throws, some for breaking the arm, and some for restraining. Here we are only going to examine two styles of standing arm bars. The first will be a basic arm bar that can be used to disarm the aggressor; the second will be an arm bar designed to bring the two combatants closer together.

As before, all the energy of the lock is controlled by the performer of the initial attack, while the defender who is performing the lock follows their partner's lead.

Basic Arm Bar

The basic arm bar can be executed from any attack. The illusion of this lock is to take the attacker off balance and lock out the elbow joint in a straight line from their body. Here the attacker is in full control of the arm and their balance by stepping into the move, bending the knees, and bending slightly from the waist. This arm bar is a good choice if you want to do a knee smash to the arm for a disarm, or if you need to take your partner down to the ground. Another disarm that is easy to do from this lock is the takeaway.

To start this technique, the attacker (**A**) can attack with any action; for this exercise, they will start with a basic diagonal down cut to the left shoulder. The unarmed defender (**B**) will block with a static high-left arm block with their left arm. Once the block is made, **B** will transport **A**'s attacking arm by bringing their right arm up and under the attacking arm and transferring it up and around to **B**'s right hip. During the transport, **B** will roll their hand into a hook and place it on **A**'s wrist while taking a small pivot step back with the right foot and shifting their upper torso to the right. **A** will take a small step forward left towards **B** with their right foot, and with bent knees will add a small bend at the waist while rolling their arm. **B** can then place their left hand on **A**'s forearm. Once the move is finished, any of the disarms described previously can be executed.

Arm Bar 2

This arm bar can be done from any attack. The goal of this move is to make it look like the defender is putting leverage on the attacker's arm and locking it behind their back to control them. Again, I stress that it is very important for the attacker to always maintain full control of their arm, and that the defender only follows their partner's actions and adds no extra tension or pressure during the action. This is a nice lock to use if you want the aggressor to face the audience or camera at a low angle. The simple takeaway disarm, the wring, or the knee-smash disarm can all be used here.

To start this technique, the attacker (**A**) can attack with any action; for this exercise, they will start with a basic diagonal down cut to the left shoulder. The defender (**B**) will block with a static high-left arm block with their left arm. Once the block is made, **B** will transport **A**'s attacking arm by bringing their right arm up and under the attacking arm and transferring it up and around. During the transport, **B** will roll their hand into a hook, placing it on **A**'s wrist. Both **A** and **B** will step forward during the transport; as **A** steps forward with their right foot, **B** steps in with the left foot toward their partner. **B** should be in front of **A**. **A** will guide the hand up and around and finish palm up. In this action, **B**'s hip should be in and close to **A**'s armpit; both of **B**'s hands can be in a relaxed grip on **A**'s wrist, or the right hand can be on **A**'s wrist while the left hand rests gently on **A**'s shoulder blade, not the shoulder joint. **B** must make sure that there is no pressure or tension in their grip so that **A** is under no stress in this move.

Shoulder Lock

An arm lock that hyperflexes or hyperrotates the shoulder joint is referred to as a shoulder lock. Again, there are many different forms of shoulder locks, especially those used in martial arts. Here we are only going to examine one, the standing shoulder lock.

As before, all energy of the lock is controlled by the performer of the initial attack, while the defender who is performing the lock follows their lead.

Standing Shoulder Lock

The goal of this move is to make it look like the defender is putting leverage on the attacker's shoulder and locking their arm behind their back to control them. Again, I stress that it is very important for the attacker to always maintain full control of their arm, and that the defender only follows their partner's actions and adds no extra tension or pressure during the action. This technique is very similar to the arm bars described earlier except that we are not locking out the elbow; we will continue around with the arm, 'locking out' the shoulder with the knife behind the attacker.

To start this technique, the attacker (**A**) can attack with any action; for this exercise, they will start with a basic diagonal down cut to the left shoulder. The defender (**B**) will block with a static high-left arm block with their left arm. Once the block is made, **B** will transport **A**'s attacking arm by bringing their right arm up and under the attacking arm and transferring it up and around. During the transport, **B** will roll their hand into a hook and place it on **A**'s wrist. **A** will guide the hand up and around while turning around, pivoting on the left foot, and stepping forward and around with the right foot. **A** will guide their hand up behind them and place the back of the hand on their lower back. **B** should be behind **A** at this moment, with their hand still gently on **A**'s arm. Once **A** finishes executing the move, **B** should put their left hand on **A**'s left shoulder. **A** should act as if the pain is in their right shoulder by raising it slightly.

Be very aware of where the knife is at all times and pay attention to the path the knife is making between the actors.

Disarms

Disarms are ways of removing the opponent's weapon to create tension, to show a character's skill, or to equalize the fight. A character may choose to do a disarm either to remove the weapon from their opponent or to take the weapon for themself. Disarms can be done by leverage, causing 'pain' to the arm/hand holding the weapon, or by simply removing the weapon with force.

Although there are many ways in which to disarm someone during a fight, here I am going to explore and walk you through what I have found to be the five most fundamental disarms for the stage and how to effectively perform them safely.

Notes on Safety

As with all techniques in this section, the one losing the knife is in full control and should never have the prop forcefully removed from their control by their partner.

When dropping a knife/dagger, always try to drop the prop flat. This helps prevent the knife from bouncing and causing damage to the prop and stage/set.

Types of prop knives and their reactions to being dropped:

Rubber knives will tend to bounce and do not make a very realistic sound when dropped. This sound issue is only a consideration for theatre, as in film and television this sound can be covered in post. Be careful during disarms, as with some actions the blade may bend and not look very realistic.

Aluminum knives, depending on their thickness, may tend to bend if dropped; thick aluminum knives will hold their shape. Another issue with aluminum is that dropping it on concrete or stone may scuff and nick the edges, so proper blade maintenance is especially needed for each take with aluminum knives.

Hard plastic or 3D-printed knives can be very fragile. Depending on the material they are made from, plastic knives can break or the blade may snap off when dropped. They also suffer the same sound issues as rubber knives.

Painted wood knives not only have the same sound issues as rubber and plastic but depending on the thickness of the blade and the wood being used, they may also tend to break. Another issue to pay attention to on wooden knives is the possibility of fractures and splintering both in the handle and blade areas.

Steel fixed-blade knives will always have a great sound when dropped but are the heaviest of all the knives. Although much sturdier than aluminum, proper blade maintenance is needing when working around concrete or stone. Also be aware that some manufactured fixed-blade knives may have a weakly welded tang that could snap when dropped multiple times.

Any kind of **folding or non-fixed-blade knife** has potential for problems when dropped. An issue I have experienced is working with folding tactical knives that have been repurposed for theatrical fighting; when these were dropped, the plastic handle has broken, sending a small piece of plastic down stage. One other common issue I have found with some folding knives is that after repeated drops, the locking mechanism may become unstable and cease to work properly. For knives like switchblades or out-the-front knives, the spring load may become damaged and the switch may no longer eject the blade properly. Although I have never experienced the following, I have heard stories where a non-fixed-blade knife has been dropped and just completely come apart on stage.

Never lose control of where your prop is going during a disarm and be aware of your surroundings at all times during the choreography. Having a prop go into the pit or audience is always bad. Rehearse the choreography to where the prop lands in the same spot every time. There is never an excuse for putting anyone in danger.

The Takeaway

The takeaway disarm is one of the easiest and most controlled methods of disarming, as the weapon transfers from one hand to another. This is especially useful when the weapon needs to shift from one combatant to the other. Another great use for using this disarm is when dealing with an audience in close proximity to the fight, such as theatre in the round.

There are three methods to doing the takeaway: from the top, palm-to-palm, and from underneath.

From the top – Taking a knife away by the blade can be done believably, as there are always areas of the blade that are not 'sharp', such as the flat side of the blade or the backside of a single-edged blade. Remember, these are theatrical weapons, so there should never be a sharp edge or point on the blade.

The attacker (**A**) holds the knife in an overhand grip. Once **A** has been restrained in either a grab or lock, the defender (**B**) uses their non-restraining hand to slide over the top (the index finger/thumb side) of **A**'s hand. This can be done with either the top or base of **B**'s hand. As **B**'s hand slides over the knife, **A** relaxes their hand enough so that **B** may be able to remove the knife safely and securely.

Deciding which way **B** will remove the knife will entirely depend on the following actions after the disarm. If **B** needs to be holding the knife in an overhand grip, **B** should use the top of their hand. If, however, **B** needs to be in an underhand grip with the knife, **B** should use the base of the hand for the disarm. This will be reversed if **A** is holding the knife in an underhand grip.

<u>Palm-to-palm</u> – The attacker (**A**) holds the knife in an overhand grip. Once **A** has been restrained in either a grab or lock, the defender (**B**) uses their non-restraining hand to slide over the front (moving from the inside wrist, over the palm of the hand, and to the fingertips) of **A**'s hand. As **B**'s hand slides over the knife, **A** relaxes their hand enough so that **B** may be able to remove the knife safely by rolling it out and grabbing hold of the knife safely and securely by the handle.

<u>From the bottom</u> – The attacker (**A**) holds the knife in an overhand grip. Once **A** has been restrained in either a grab or lock, the defender (**B**) uses their non-restraining hand to slide over the bottom (the fourth finger/small finger side) of **A**'s hand. This can be done with either the top or base of **B**'s hand. As **B**'s hand slides over the knife, **A** relaxes their hand enough so that **B** may be able to remove the knife safely and securely.

Deciding which way **B** will remove the knife will entirely depend on the following actions after the disarm. If **B** needs to be holding the knife in an overhand grip, **B** should use the bottom of their hand. If, however, **B** needs to be in an underhand grip with the knife, **B** should use the top of the hand for the disarm. This will be reversed if **A** is holding the knife in an underhand grip.

The Forearm Push

The forearm push is a simple disarm that can be used either to take the weapon away from the attacker or to remove the weapon from the fight. In this action, once the attacker's arm is in a lock or hold, the defender pushes their free forearm against the flat of the attacker's weapon and, using leverage, pushes the dagger towards the attacker. At this point, the defender can either take the weapon with their free hand or allow it to fall to the ground.

The attacker (**A**) holds the knife in an overhand grip. Once **A** has been restrained in either a hold or lock, the defender (**B**) uses their non-restraining hand's forearm to push against the side of **A**'s blade. **B** pushes their forearm towards **A**. **A** relaxes their hand enough so that **B** may be able to remove the knife safely and securely. This technique can be performed with the knife point up or down, depending on what position **A** is in at the end of the hold or lock.

The Wring

The wring is a simple disarm where the attacker is in full control of their weapon the entire time. As the defender executes the wring, the attacker simply acts the pain and drops the knife flat on the ground. This is a good disarm to use from an arm bar or shoulder lock. Just be careful not to drop the knife on your partner's foot!

Once the attacker (**A**) has been restrained in either a hold or lock, the defender (**B**) uses their hands in a relaxed fashion to mimic wringing of **A**'s forearm and hand. **B**'s hands should be on the forearm and wrist in a relaxed grip, and each hand moved in an opposite direction. This action makes it look like you are twisting the hand and forearm in opposite directions, causing the hand to lose grip of the knife. **A** drops the blade down to the ground with a focus on the blade landing flat. This technique can be performed with **A** and **B** adding a small bounce to the arm to look like more force is being used.

I have used this often in opera, where an attack is coming in and **B** blocks the attack with their left arm, grabs the forearm of **A**, and performs a twisting action that mimics the wring but uses only one hand, as **B** is usually holding someone or something in their other hand.

The Knee-Smash

Knee smashes are a great way to add more dynamics to a fight by involving more body work into the action. In this disarm, the defender 'smashes' their knee into the attacker's forearm, causing them to drop the knife. This is an acted percussion, as the attacker is in full control of the action and in full control of making contact with the defender's thigh.

Once the attacker (**A**) has been restrained in a hold or lock, the defender (**B**) places their hands in a relaxed fashion on **A**'s forearm. **A** takes control as **B** follows the action. **A** will lift their arm slightly; this is the signal to **B** to lift a knee. **A** then proceeds to bring their forearm down on the top of **B**'s thigh and drop the knife, with a focus on the blade landing flat. This technique can be performed with **A** and **B** adding a small bounce to look like more force is being used.

The Object-Smash

Like the knee-smash, using objects and surfaces are great ways to add dynamics to fights. These are especially useful for video, as you can close in on the action. The same principles are applied here as in the knee-smash, as the attacker is in full control of the action and leads the momentum that the defender follows with a light grip.

Objects can include walls, tables, chair backs, and bar tops. Other objects, such as blunt weapons or breakaway bottles, can be used across the forearm or hand. Make sure you are using stage combat-appropriate items.

Closing Comments

There are all kinds of ways to disarm someone for a show. Experiment with different ways that help tell your story. Just be safe with your actions, and as stated earlier, always be aware of your knife, where it is moving, or where it is falling.

8

THREATS, CUTS, MURDERS, AND SUICIDE

In this chapter, we are going to explore some of the more common uses of knives and daggers outside of fighting, such as the actions of threats, murder, and suicide. These are actions that happen in many plays, operas, or stories in which you will be working with a knife/dagger. We see these all the time in scenes such as Juliet's death in *Romeo and Juliet*, Don José killing Carmen, Tosca killing Scarpia, Julius Caesar's death, Cio-Cio-san's suicide in *Madama Butterfly*, and countless threats and hostage moments in television shows and movies. These moments allow for the stakes of the scene to be raised to a high moment. Some give us our final payoff, others set the tone for what is to come, and some are just used to build tension in the story. Whichever option you are working with, know that a poorly performed scene will ruin the effect you are going for or worse yet, they could cause injuries and accidents if not properly executed or if using the wrong type of prop weapon.

DOI: 10.4324/9781003147862-8

Although we covered safety in the first chapter, I am repeating this here in case you decided to jump straight to this chapter or are reading it again for a refresher. As always, safety should be your top priority when working with any form of violence. This is doubly true when placing a prop weapon on another person in a threatening manner. Safety precautions must include mental safety for the actors as well. As a director, choreographer, teacher, or performer, we will never know who is dealing with trauma, but we can use safe practices that will help minimize risk when working with performers. This is especially true for any scenes that deal with threating someone with a weapon in a non-fight-related scene.

As a director or as a choreographer, it is not our job to be a therapist for our performers, but it is our job to keep them safe. When approaching any scene work with violence, or threats of violence, take a moment to sit down with your performers and go over the action verbally first. Check with your performers to see if they are comfortable with the actions you described and the situation as you will choreograph it. Remember, their safety is your first concern; you can always work around someone's boundaries, but you never want to cross them. Pay attention to their body language in the conversation – many performers feel that they always have to say "yes" to a director or choreographer, but body language can easily give someone away. It may be that they don't want to seem as a 'problem actor' or 'difficult to work with'. Sometimes, you may want to talk to them individually in the rehearsal room, where if they are uncomfortable talking openly about an issue, they can feel safer addressing the choreography without additional people listening in. As a director or choreographer, it is never our job to judge what someone has experienced in the past or to push actions upon them that they are having emotional difficulty with. Sometimes performers may not be aware of an emotional or trauma-related trigger until it happens. If that happens, take a break, let the performer collect themselves and when they are ready, start over, talk through the action, and if needed, look for ways to adjust the choreography to avoid the newly discovered boundary. Never shame a performer for their boundaries, and never assume that those boundaries stay consistent.

Note: Never bring a prop weapon, even a soft rubber weapon, near your partner's face, especially around the eyes!

Threating With a Knife

In this section, we will look at how to threaten someone with a knife. The two most common ways to threaten someone with a knife are from the front or from behind.

To threaten from the front

As in all actions with contact, the victim is in full control while the attacker follows their lead. The attacker (**A**) will first use their empty hand to "grab" the victim (**B**). This can be done by placing the hand on the shoulder, upper arm, or wherever best fits the story. Once contact is made, **B** can then bring the weapon close to **A**. **B** can then place their hand, either palm down or palm up, on **A**'s upper chest. In this situation, the knife is not touching **A**'s throat but can give the illusion of contact and a sense of danger.

If there is a lot of struggling with this scene, I recommend that **A** grab hold of **B**'s hand to keep it in a secure position while the struggle happens. The grabbing of the hand can be done with either one or both hands. This prevents **B**'s hand from slipping and maintains the safety of the fight. The illusion here is to make it look like **A** is resisting or trying to pull **B**'s hand away, while it is in fact clamping the hand to **A**'s body to prevent it from sliding up towards the neck or from **A** pulling away from the knife and creating a gap between **A** and **B**, thus losing all intention in the choreography.

To threaten from behind

The knife threat from behind is probably the most common knife threat used, especially in film and television. Here the aggressor (**A**) will stand behind or slightly to the side of the victim (**B**) while holding a knife to their neck. As before, we always want the victim to be in control of the situation while the attacker follows their lead.

The action starts with **A** placing a hand on **B**'s shoulder or other area as story dictates. This serves two reasons; the first is to give spatial awareness to the victim, who does not have eye contact with the attacker, and the second is to create the illusion of control of the attacker.

Next, in a large open action, **B** brings the knife around **A**'s body to the front. Here we use a big action so that **A** can see the approaching weapon and react to the situation. This also allows **A** to guide the action in by pulling the hand/arm into their upper chest, as if they are fighting against it. Like before, **A** is in full control and will manipulate **B**'s hand/arm during the action. Another safety precaution that can be used here is to have **B**'s body supporting **A**'s body. Here **B** acts as a wall for **A** to press up against with their back, so that spatial awareness is maintained during the struggle and the illusion of control is maintained.

With smaller bladed knives, such as folding knives, **B** can "thumb the edge" to create an extra level of safety. However, this technique only works in theatre and does not read well on camera. To thumb the edge, **B** places their thumb on the 'edge' side of the blade, between the knife and **A**'s neck. This prevents the actual blade, especially a metal blade, from touching **A**, which is particularly useful in any situation where **A** is struggling and **B** must maintain contact or maintain the threat.

Stabbing Someone

Whether accidental or on purpose, stabs are often used in storytelling. They can be a physical act to end emotional suffering or bring resolution to a fight; they can be used to create tension, set up how 'bad' a character is, or even be used as a comic moment. Whichever style you are going for in your production, you must always be aware of the safety issues when working stabs. In this section, we will explore the various ways to stab someone, with a focus on theatrical settings. These same techniques can be used in film with just smart camera angles and added special or post-effects. With all stabs, there are two ways of performing the action. The first is the fast 'in and out', where the stab action happens quickly and is immediately withdrawn from the victim – think Julius Caesar's death, a shower scene stabbing, or a prison shanking. The second is the 'stab and stay', where once the victim is stabbed, the weapon remains in the wound with either the attacker letting go of the weapon or holding on while watching the victim — this is used in *Carmen*, *Othello*, and many others.

Please review the section about stabs and cuts before starting this unit. Be aware of your stage and staging of the scene to pick the best action for the moment. As with all actions in this book, start slow and master the actions before speeding up to performance speed.

Staging note about stabs: The performer will need to cover/mask the wound immediately after the action. This hides the fact that there is no hole in the clothing or actual wound in the character.

Stabbing someone from the front

In this action, the attacker (**A**) is facing the victim (**B**) during the stab.

Method #1: In and Out Flat

Here the actors are facing each other flat with the audience. **A** performs a thrust with the weapon forward into the empty space between **B**'s torso and arm and pulls the weapon back quickly. This move is all about timing on both partners' parts, as **B** must react appropriately and **A** cannot go so fast as both the audience and their partner will miss the action. **B** can then pop a blood pack (if provided) or react upstage. For added safety, **A** can first place their unarmed hand on **B**'s shoulder to maintain the proper distance.

This type of attack can target anywhere on **B**'s body as long as the weapon has a clear path upstage. The common issue with this action is the stab may look bad when the attacker's knife passes all the way through the victim because of an overreach of **A**'s attack.

Method #2: In and Out Victim Upstage

Here the actors are facing each other, with the victim of the stab upstage of the attacker. **A** performs a thrust with the weapon and as the knife closes in, **A** turns the knife flat with **B**'s torso, then pulls back quickly while straightening out the weapon. This move works very similarly to a contact punch to the stomach. Pay attention to each other and make sure that when **A** reacts to the stab by bending over, there is no accidental contact such as a headbutt. This move is all about timing on both partners' parts, as **B** must react appropriately and **A** cannot go so fast as both the audience and their partner will miss the action. **B** can then react. For added safety, **A** can first place their unarmed hand on **B**'s shoulder to maintain the proper distance.

Method #3: In and Out Victim Downstage

Of all the 'in and out' attacks, this is the safest to perform. Here the actors are facing each other, with the victim of the stab downstage of the attacker. **A** performs a thrust with the weapon and as the knife closes in, **A** stops the action short, then pulls back quickly. This move is about timing on **B**'s part, as they must react appropriately. **B** can then pop a blood pack and react by turning downstage.

Method #1: Stab and Stay Flat

A performs a thrust with the weapon forward into the empty space between **B**'s torso and arm and holds the weapon in place. **B** can then pop a blood pack and grab hold of the weapon/hand/arm of **A** while reacting to the action.

Method #2: Stab and Stay Victim Upstage

A performs a thrust with the weapon and as the knife closes in, **A** turns the knife flat with **B**'s torso. An added movement can be made as **A** closes distance with B, where both actors are in an embrace. **B** can then pop a blood pack before **A** steps back. A note to watch for with this action is to make sure the blade is flat with both combatants' torsos so that when distance is closed, the blade of the weapon is not a physical threat to either performer. **B** can take control of the weapon, if desired, and hold it to their body, as **A** lets go.

Method #3: Stab and Stay Victim Downstage

A performs a thrust with the weapon and as the knife closes in, **A** stops the action short, then closes the distance and places the weapon between themselves. **B** can take control of the weapon, if desired, and hold it to their body as **A** lets go.

Stabbing someone from behind

All the previous stabs can be done from behind. In these actions, the attacker (**A**) is facing the victim (**B**), who has their back turned to **A** during the stab.

The best way to perform an action without eye contact between the combatants in live theatre is to use a vocal cue along with a physical contact before the action. A vocal cue can be a word or a sound that cues the victim that the action is about to be performed. The physical contact can be simply placing a hand on the victim's shoulder or any other agreed-upon area.

Stabbing someone in the back from the front

In this technique, both performers are facing each other and are usually in an embrace of some type. This is typically performed with one actor upstage of the other, so that either the victim's face or the attacker's face can be seen by the audience. In film, we can just cut between the two in closeups. The attack itself is very simple; it will either come from a high line or a low line.

Things to consider: Who do you want to be the focus? Do you want to focus on the killer or the victim? Whose face do we want the audience to see? What is the height difference between the performers? If one is much shorter than the other, we may not want the shorter performer upstage of the taller performer. What happens immediately after? Do they remain in an embrace that takes them both to the floor? Does the attacker just let the victim fall to the floor? What happens to the knife after the action? Can the victim take the knife with them, do we let the knife drop to the floor after, or do we want the attacker to hold the knife while the victim is on the ground before them? In *Carmen*'s end scene, we can create two very different moments with Carmen's death. In the first, we can have both Don José and Carmen collapse to the ground together, Don José keeping Carmen in his arms and embracing her as she dies. In the other, we can have Don José remove the knife as Carmen collapses in front of him, Don José standing above her body as she lays on the ground dying.

Method #1: In and Out Victim Downstage

High attack coming down in reverse grip between the neck and shoulder.

Here the actors are standing, with the victim of the stab (**B**) downstage of the attacker (**A**), facing the audience. **A** performs a downward stab in reverse grip, and as the knife closes in, **A** opens the space between themselves and **B** and turns the knife flat, horizontally with **B**'s torso, and slides the knife between their bodies, only making contact with the flat of the hand. This move is all about timing on both partners' parts, as **A** provides a physical cue with the hand contact and **B** must react appropriately. As the action is made, there is a small pause before **A** pulls the blade back, allowing **B** to react a second time.

Low attack coming up into the stomach or ribcage.

Here the actors are standing, with the victim of the stab (**B**) downstage of the attacker (**A**), facing the audience. **A** performs an upward stab in either normal or reverse grip, and as the knife closes in, **A** opens the space between themselves and **B** and turns the knife flat, vertically with **B**'s torso, and slides the knife between their bodies, only making contact with the flat of the hand. This move is all about timing on both partners' parts, as **A** provides a physical cue with the hand contact and **B** must react appropriately. As the action is made, there is a small pause before **A** pulls the blade back, allowing **B** to react a second time.

Method #2: In and Out Victim Upstage

High attack coming down in reverse grip between the neck and shoulder.

Here the actors are standing, with the victim of the stab (**B**) upstage of the attacker (**A**), facing the audience. **A** performs a downward stab in reverse grip, and as the knife closes in, **A**, overextending behind **B**, turns the knife flat, horizontally with **B**'s torso and behind the shoulder blades, only making contact with the flat of the hand. This move is all about timing on both partners' parts, as **A** provides a physical cue with the hand contact and **B** must react appropriately. As the action is made, there is a small pause before **A** pulls the blade back, allowing **B** to react a second time.

Low attack coming up into the stomach or ribcage.

Here the actors are standing, with the victim of the stab (**B**) upstage of the attacker (**A**), facing the audience. **A** performs an upward stab in either normal or reverse grip, and as the knife closes in, **A**, overextending behind **B**, turns the knife flat, vertically behind **B**'s torso, only making contact with the flat of the hand. This move is all about timing on both partners' parts, as **A** provides a physical cue with the hand contact and **B** must react appropriately. As the action is made, there is a small pause before **A** pulls the blade back, allowing **B** to react a second time.

This can also be performed with the knife between the two performers, as it is in the Victim Downstage.

Method #1: Stab and Stay Victim Downstage

High attack coming down in reverse grip between the neck and shoulder.

Here the actors are standing, with the victim of the stab (**B**) downstage of the attacker (**A**), facing the audience. **A** performs a downward stab in reverse grip, and as the knife closes in, **A** opens space between themselves and **B** and turns the knife flat, horizontally with **B**'s torso, and slides the knife between their bodies, only making contact with the flat of the hand. This move is all about timing on both partners' parts, as **A** provides a physical cue with the hand contact and **B** must react appropriately.

Low attack coming up into the stomach or ribcage.

Here the actors are standing, with the victim of the stab (**B**) downstage of the attacker (**A**), facing the audience. **A** performs an upward stab in either normal or reverse grip, and as the knife closes in, **A** opens space between themselves and **B** and turns the knife flat, vertically with **B**'s torso, and slides the knife between their bodies, only making contact with the flat of the hand. This move is all about timing on both partners' parts, as **A** provides a physical cue with the hand contact and **B** must react appropriately.

Method #2: Stab and Stay Victim Upstage

High attack coming down in reverse grip between the neck and shoulder.

Here the actors are standing, with the victim of the stab (**B**) upstage of the attacker (**A**), facing the audience. **A** performs a downward stab in reverse grip, and as the knife closes in, **A,** overextending behind **B**, turns the knife flat, horizontally with **B**'s torso and behind the shoulder blades, and only makes contact with the flat of the hand. This move is all about timing on both partners' parts, as **A** provides a physical cue with the hand contact and **B** must react appropriately.

Low attack coming up into the stomach or ribcage.

Here the actors are standing, with the victim of the stab (**B**) upstage of the attacker (**A**), facing the audience. **A** performs an upward stab in either normal or reverse grip, and as the knife closes in, **A,** overextending behind **B**, turns the knife flat, vertically behind **B**'s torso, and only makes contact with the flat of the hand. This move is all about timing on both partners' parts, as **A** provides a physical cue with the hand contact and **B** must react appropriately.

This can also be performed with the knife between the two performers, as it is in the Victim Downstage from earlier in this chapter.

Ground Work

Occasionally, you will need to stage a stabbing or a threat where the combatants are on the ground. Ground fighting always presents challenges, and adding a weapon to the mix can complicate things even more. As always, work slowly and safely while learning and building the choreography, and communicate with both actors constantly about boundaries and comfort levels.

To Threaten on the Ground

The trick to this is to make sure the action can be seen by the audience and that the attacker (**A**) is in a firm mounted position, stable and in balance. As in all actions with contact, the victim is in full control while the attacker follows their lead. **A** will first use their empty hand to "grab" the victim (**B**). This can be done by placing the hand on the shoulder, upper arm, or wherever best fits the story. Once contact is made, **B** can then bring the weapon close to **A**. **B** can then place their hand, either palm down or palm up, on **A**'s upper chest. In this situation, the knife is not touching **A**'s throat but can give the illusion of contact and a sense of danger.

If there is a lot of struggling with this scene, I recommend that **A** grab hold of **B**'s hand to keep it in a secure position while the struggle happens. The grabbing of the hand can be done with either one or both hands. This prevents **B**'s hand from slipping and maintains the safety of the fight. The illusion here is to make it look like **A** is resisting or trying to pull **B**'s hand away, while it is in fact clamping the hand to **A**'s body to prevent it from sliding up towards the neck or from **A** pulling away from the knife and creating a gap between **A** and **B**, thus losing all intention in the choreography.

Overhand Stab

This is a technique that I very rarely ever use, as there is not much need to do this on stage. Most stabs from a ground position are going to be the underhand stab. I wanted to include it just in case you may ever need it.

This starts in a solid mounted position from the attacker (**A**). **A** can either be sitting astride their partner (**B**) or be between their legs. **A** needs to draw the knife back enough for the audience to see it. **A** will then bring the knife down and next to **B**'s torso, on the upstage side. This is best performed with the actors horizontal to the audience, with the knife hand upstage. **B** can then react by sharply contracting their core.

Underhand Stab

This is the most common type of mounted stab, as it is probably the most dramatic style of stabbing. This can be staged with both actors horizontal to the audience, or where the mounted attacker is facing the audience, with their partner's head downstage. If wanting to use implied violence, the attacker's back can be to the audience, and the performer on the ground would sell the pain.

This starts in a solid mounted position from the attacker (**A**). **A** can either be sitting astride their partner (**B**) or be between their legs. **A** needs to draw the knife up enough for the audience to see it. **A** can be holding the knife with one hand or both hands. **A** performs a stab with the weapon, and as the knife closes in, **A** turns the knife flat with **B**'s torso, then pulls back quickly while straightening out the weapon. Unlike the previous stab, this time as the knife comes down towards **B**, the blade is laid flat vertically with the torso, between the chest and hips, along the stomach. This move is all about timing on both partners' parts, as **B** must react appropriately and **A** cannot go so fast as both the audience and their partner will miss the action. **B** can then react with their head and shoulders, as reacting with the core may change the distance.

Counter-Cutting

Cuts can be added to blocks and transports to add another layer of dynamics to the choreography. These actions are quick slices to the extremities, such as the arms, or body cuts. The trick in the choreography is to make them appear seamless and part of the action.

Types of Cuts

Slice – A slice is drawing the edge or tip of the knife in a deliberate manner across the skin to open it up. Most common slices are made with scalpels or razor blades. Actions can include cutting open of the wrist, surgery, or throat cuts (think *Sweeney Todd: The Demon Barber of Fleet Street*).

Chop – A chop is a strong, quick action, usually performed with the middle of the blade's edge. Chops are usually done with wide blades, such as butcher's knives, cleavers, and machetes. Think of food preparation or the removal of a finger.

Draw-cut – A draw-cut is any cut with the edge of the blade as it is pulled (drawn) across the skin. This is usually the most common cut in knife fighting.

Push-cut – A push-cut is any cut with the edge of the blade as it is pushed across the skin. This would be like trying to stab the target but missing, and instead cutting the side as you push your knife forward.

Hack – A hack is a bigger, stronger, and less precise action than the chop and is usually repeated several times.

Rip – A rip is a tearing of the skin or clothing. This can be done with a dull blade, a jagged blade like a hand saw, or any object that can puncture the skin and be drawn across it.

Performing Cuts

There are two ways to perform cuts: contact and non-contact.

Contact cuts are where the prop knife actually makes contact with the performer's skin or costume. Either the blunted edge of the blade or the flat of the blade can be used to make contact with the performer. Even though these are contact cuts, the pressure of the contact should be light and not forceful. It is extremely important when doing any type of contact action with knives that the blade be free from any nicks or burrs, that all edges are dulled, and that the point is rounded off to a safe level. All wooden weapons need to be checked for nicks or splintered areas, and hard plastic knives need to be checked for any nicks that may catch the skin or costume. (Review blade maintenance at the start of the book.)

Non-contact cuts are where the action of the cut is implied but the blade does not come into contact with the performer nor their costume.

Cuts to the Extremities

Here we will perform all blocks with the left arm and counter-cut the arm with the right. The cut can be performed either in an upward or downward action, whichever works best for the choreography or the flow. In this exercise, I will describe one action for the counter-cuts, but like the cuts you learned in an earlier chapter, there are always variations to the actions. Also, you can either perform a contact cut or a non-contact cut. Reactions to these cuts will be found at the end of the section.

1. As the attacker (**A**) starts the actions with the first cut to the left shoulder of the blocker (**B**), **B** can then perform a static block to **A**'s forearm with the back of their forearm. **B** then counter-cuts across **A**'s arm, between the block and **A**'s torso, with a diagonal down cut from right to left.
2. As **A** cuts to the right shoulder, **B** pivots to the right, then performs a static block to **A**'s forearm with the back of their forearm. **B** then counter-cuts across **A**'s forearm, between the block and **A**'s torso, with a diagonal down cut from left to right.
3. As **A** cuts to the left hip, **B** then performs a static block to **A**'s forearm with the back of their forearm. **B** then counter-cuts across **A**'s forearm, between the block and **A**'s torso, with a diagonal up cut from right to left.
4. As **A** cuts to the right hip, **B** pivots to the right, then performs a static block to **A**'s forearm with the back of their forearm. **B** then

counter-cuts across **A**'s forearm, between the block and **A**'s torso, with a diagonal up cut from left to right.

5. As **A** stabs/thrusts in a pronated action to the left side, **B** performs a static block to **A**'s forearm with the back of their forearm. **B** then counter-cuts across **A**'s forearm, between the block and **A**'s torso, with a horizontal cut from right to left.

6. As **A** cuts from **B**'s left to right on the midline, **B** performs a static block to **A**'s forearm with the back of their forearm. **B** then counter-cuts across **A**'s forearm, between the block and **A**'s torso, with a horizontal cut from left to right.

7. As **A** stabs/thrusts in a supinated action to the right side, **B** pivots to the right, then performs a static block to **A**'s forearm with the back of their forearm. **B** then counter-cuts across **A**'s forearm, between the block and **A**'s torso, with a horizontal cut from right to left.

8. As **A** cuts from **B**'s right to left on the midline, **B** pivots to the right, then performs a static block to **A**'s forearm with the back of their forearm. **B** then counter-cuts across **A**'s forearm, between the block and **A**'s torso, with a horizontal cut from left to right.

9. As **A** cuts down, **B** performs a static block to **A**'s forearm with the back of their forearm. **B** then counter-cuts across **A**'s forearm, between the block and **A**'s torso, with a diagonal up cut from right to left.

10. As **A** attacks with a forward stab action to center line, **B** performs a static block to **A**'s forearm with the back of their forearm as **B** displaces towards the right (or displaces left if cross-blocking with the left arm). **B** then counter-cuts across **A**'s forearm, between the block and **A**'s torso, with a horizontal cut.

Cuts to the Torso

Here, as described previously, you can perform all blocks with the left arm and perform the counter-cut, with the exception now being that instead of cutting to the arm, you can counter-cut to the torso. The cuts can target any available part of the body and can be performed either in an upward, downward, or horizontal action – whichever works best for the choreography or the flow. When cutting to the torso, I prefer to always use the flat of the blade if I am going to be making a contact cut. I have found that this prevents, but does not totally eliminate, the chance of any accidental snags on clothing or skin.

Reactions to Cuts

Reactions are an essential part of any theatrical fight or, for that matter, any scene work between two or more performers. When a character is injured, the performer must react appropriately to the character's level of injury for it to be believed by the audience. Now the reason I say it that way is because the reaction needs to fit the violence, the character, and the style. Over-the-top reactions are great if you are doing a comedy, just as underselling the reaction can be funny or can show how stoic a character is or how little they react to pain. However, in most cases, you will want your characters to show or at least react to the pain during a fight.

Cut Reactions

Reacting to simple cuts that are not too deep or are not debilitating is done by allowing the injured area to follow the flow of the attack, along with a vocal reaction to the pain.

If **A**, while blocking **B**'s high left attack with a static block, cuts a diagonal high right to low left cut on **B**'s attacking arm, **B** can allow the arm to follow the energy of the cut down, then pull the arm into their body and cover the injury with the left hand.

If the attack is to the leg, the victim can either turn the leg in or out, depending on the direction of the cut.

If the cut is to the torso, allow the body to turn with the action, in the same direction of the cut. The victim must make a vocal reaction to the injury, and then they can cover it with their non-weapon hand to continue to sell the injury.

For deep cuts across the stomach or any area, there should be a bit more physicality added to the reaction. The first part of the reaction should be a collapse of the body towards the cut while turning with the direction of the action. A deeper vocal reaction is needed, much like one that would accompany a punch to the stomach. The victim can either drop down to a knee or completely collapse on the floor or on a nearby object.

Stab Reactions

When a quick stab happens, whether it's pulled out or left in, the body needs to react in a different way than reacting to cuts.

If the stab is pulled out: As the stab happens, the victim will react by having their whole body move towards the pain and the direction of the stab. When the blade is removed, the body follows the direction of the withdrawal.

If **A**, while blocking **B**'s high left attack with a static block, stabs to **B**'s stomach, **B** will follow the energy of the stab by reacting like a punch to the stomach, with the middle of the torso moving back with the action and the body moving towards the pain. As **A** withdraws the blade, **B**'s torso should shift forward, following the action of the withdrawal. **B** would make vocal reactions to both the stab and the removal.

B could reverse these actions if they are stabbed in the back from behind, by throwing their stomach/sternum area forward with the stab and then collapsing down to their stomach, curving their back as the knife is removed.

If the knife is not removed, **B** would continue the collapse around the knife and either take control of the knife (making sure it stays in place), allowing **A** to step away if needed; or if **A** maintains control of the knife, then **B** would continue to a point where they can support themselves on **A**.

A note about covering the injury: I have found that it is useful to cover the injury as soon as possible. This helps with a couple of things – the first being to hide that no actual cut was made to the skin or costume and the second being that it helps sell the pain of the action and may give the audience and characters a brief moment to acknowledge the injury. Also, if the performer is using a blood pack, this is a great way to apply or utilize it.

Suicide

Suicide is always a tricky subject to talk about, and even more so to stage. Remember to always approach and address the scene seriously and respectfully. Unfortunately, many people either know someone who has attempted or committed suicide or have attempted suicide themselves. It will be easy for your performers to use humor to deflect the uncomfortable issue of suicide; just remember to keep everyone focused and keep checking in with the actors while working on these scenes. If someone needs a break, let them step away and collect themselves. Always talk about the actions in clean, technical terminology, always explaining that this is theatrical and that the actor is at no risk of injury when the actions are performed correctly. Again, always respect an actor's boundaries and work with them to establish a strong scene that they can perform and repeat.

NOTE: Before I even start this section, let me just repeat that **I do not recommend ever using a retractable blade knife or dagger.** These types of knives are very dangerous and can cause injury. It is all too easy for the blade mechanism to get stuck or trapped, so that the blade does not retract or collapse properly and the knife actually penetrates the performer.

Stabbing Yourself

Self-stabbings and suicides are techniques that are very common in storylines – including *Romeo and Juliet, Carousel,* and *Madama Butterfly* – and are easy and safe to perform when done properly. Depending on your production, many of these can be done without the use of any fake blood.

As stated at the top of this chapter, if you are working on a film, all cuts and stabbings can be created either with the help of practical special effects or with computer-generated imagery (CGI). However, live performance does not have those options, and here we will look at how to create the illusion of self-stabs and cuts for theatre.

Stabbing Yourself in the Stomach

From Samurai to Juliet, the stomach stab is the go-to self-stab for characters on stage. As with most theatrical combat, this is about illusion and sleight-of-hand technique.

The first method is with the actor facing the audience. The actor, holding the knife in a reverse grip, creates the illusion of plunging the knife into their stomach with a downward motion. This is best when done with both hands but can be done with a single hand.

During the downward action of the knife, the actor tilts the knife in towards their forearm and presses the flat of the blade against their inside forearm. Then they place their forearm on their stomach, with the handle of the knife a few inches away from the center of their body.

The actor can either leave it there as they die, or they can remove it in a reverse action, exposing the blade on the 'withdrawal' and covering the 'wound' with the other hand.

The second method of this is with the actor in profile to the audience.

During the downward action of the knife, same as before, the actor can then bring their arm straight into the downstage side of their body, knife flat against their forearm, giving the illusion of a straight stab inwards.

To add a blood effect to this, the actor can either have a blood pouch in their empty hand and crush it as they grab the wound, or they can have a blood pouch under their clothing that they break after the stab.

Seppuku

Ritualized suicide (or assisted suicide) with cutting the stomach open is called *seppuku* in Japan and can also be referred to as *hara-kiri*. Although highly associated with male samurai, females also did a form of seppuku where the knife enters the neck and cuts the arteries. The opera *Madama Butterfly* ends with Cio-Cio-san's suicide, which can either be staged behind a wall or on stage in front of the audience.

Male Seppuku

The samurai, typically dressed in a white kimono and kneeling on a white cushion, would begin the ritual of seppuku. In front of the samurai would be a small wooden table with the *kozuka* – the ritual blade. The samurai would write a *jisei*, a death poem, before the final act. Witnesses would be seated to the side and an assistant, known as a *kaishakunin*, would stand to the left of the samurai. The *kaishakunin* would assist the samurai by ending their suffering with a fatal cut to the neck with a sword.

To stage this, use the same technique as that for stabbing yourself in the stomach, described previously, with a horizontal movement of the hands after the "stab".

Female Seppuku

Female ritual suicide was practiced by the wives of samurai who have performed seppuku, brought dishonor, or to prevent their capture. Before committing suicide, a woman would often tie her knees together so her body would be found in a dignified pose, even with the actions of the body during death.

To stage this, there are two methods that can be used:

Method 1

Using the same technique as a self-stab with the audience in profile; however, here the actress will face the audience with the knife arm turned upstage (right hand lowering the knife into the left shoulder/neck side) and slide the knife arm down, making it look like she is stabbing the knife between her neck and shoulder.

Method 2

Using a sheath secured to the body under the clothing, the actress can slide the knife into the sheath, and let go of the knife as she collapses on the stage.

Closing Comments

We covered a lot of information in this chapter. Please take your time learning these actions to get them down nice and smooth. As always, start slow and take your time building up to performance speed. Remember to keep your and your partner's safety the focus of all the techniques. If you are directing these actions, talk with your performers about the actions and check in with them throughout the process. Try to work in the performance costumes as soon as possible, as some moves may work great while the performers are in jeans and shirts but become more complicated or need to be altered once the actors are in their costumes. A reminder that performers may still need to sing or speak after a fight, especially in opera, and if they are out of breath and cannot sing or speak, the flow of the story is disrupted.

9

ADDING FLAIR

In this chapter, we are going to explore some techniques that add an additional level of flair to choreography. These actions build upon the previous sections, so please make sure you have the basic techniques down before working on these actions. We will also explore different ways of adding elements to your fight, such as capes, towels, double knives, and hooking with the knife block. We will also examine ways to perform knife throws both in the technique of the action and in the staging. We will end the chapter by looking at ways to add flair to changing your grip on the knife and in transferring the knife from one hand to another.

Off-Hand Protection

One of the easiest techniques to use to enhance a fight is to adopt off-hand protection. Using part of a costume – such as a cape, cloak, jacket, or towel – will give the unarmed hand some defensive protection. The combatant can either hold the item or wrap it around their arm (see Figure 9.1).

DOI: 10.4324/9781003147862-9

Figure 9.1 Holding or Wrapping a Jacket

The left arm can then be used to block incoming attacks or be used as a distraction toward your opponent.

This method of fighting is very common in the choreography for *Carmen*, in the knife fight between Don José and Escamillo.

Towel Versus Knife

A knife versus a towel can be a very exciting combo to create. We see this in *The Bourne Ultimatum* during the fight scene between Bourne (Matt Damon) and Desh (Joey Ansah), when the two combatants are in the bathroom. Desh picks up a straight razor, while Bourne grabs a hand towel. The combo part of the fight only lasts about eight seconds on screen, but it shows the dynamics of how their fight is evolving, from guns to empty hands to found objects and then to knife and towel. Bourne disarms Desh and proceeds to (spoiler) choke him out with the towel.

The towel can be used in multiple ways. It can be wrapped around the hand/wrist area, such as in the previous section on off-hand protection, it can be wrapped around the entire arm if big enough, or it can be held in the hand and used like a cloak/jacket.

The towel can also be used in both hands as a defensive block against incoming attacks and used to trap the attacking hand/arm.

Here we will perform all blocks with the towel held in both hands.

1. As the attacker (**A**) starts the actions with the first cut to the left shoulder of the blocker (**B**), **B** can then extend the arms high forward left, with the left hand lower than the right hand, catching the attack on the towel.
2. As **A** cuts to the right shoulder, **B** pivots to the right and extends the arms high forward right, with the right hand lower than the left hand, catching the attack on the towel.
3. As **A** cuts to the left hip, **B** can then extend the arms low forward left, with the left hand higher than the right hand, catching the attack on the towel.
4. As **A** cuts to the right hip, **B** pivots right and extends the arms low forward right, with the left hand higher than the right hand, catching the attack on the towel.
5. As **A** stabs/thrusts in a pronated action to the left side, **B** extends the arms forward left, with the left hand lower than the right hand, catching the attack on the towel.
6. As **A** cuts from **B**'s left to right on the midline, **B** extends the arms forward left, with the left hand lower than the right hand, catching the attack on the towel.
7. As **A** stabs/thrusts in a supinated action to the right side, **B** pivots right and extends the arms forward right, with the right hand lower than the left hand, catching the attack on the towel.
8. As **A** cuts from **B**'s right to left on the midline, **B** pivots right and extends the arms forward right, with the right hand lower than the left hand, catching the attack on the towel.
9. As **A** cuts down, **B** extends both arms up, catching the attack on the towel.
10. As **A** attacks with a forward stab action to center line, **B** extends the arms forward with either the left or right hand in high position, depending on which direction **B** displaces. For example, if **B** displaces right, then the right hand would be in high position, catching the attack on the towel.

Hooking With the Knife

When blocking an attack with the knife hand, if the knife is being held in reverse or ice pick grip, the knife can be used to hook and control the arm. We see this in *John Wick*, *The Man from Nowhere*, and *The Raid 2*, just to name a few. I will explain this action using four of the bind transports from the active blocks section to demonstrate these actions.

Reminder: A bind is a checking action made on the opponent's hand, arm, or leg, executed by blocking the attack and then moving it diagonally to the opposite quadrant (i.e., from the inside high to the outside low, or outside high to inside low, etc.). Here, we will hook the knife to "catch and control" the partner's attack.

Notes on Safety:

Use the flat of the blade when hooking, and always keep the knife relaxed while hooking and manipulating your partner's arm. Never create a vice-like grip between your knife and your arm while trapping your partner; this will allow your partner's arm to rotate safely through the action. This will also allow them to remove their arm, should there be any problems.

1. As the attacker (**A**) starts the actions with the first cut to the left shoulder of the blocker (**B**), **B** can do a small pivot to the right and block **A**'s forearm with the back of their right forearm by rotating the palm of the hand inside. Once the block is made, the knife will hook over **A**'s wrist, while circling the arm counterclockwise and manipulating **A**'s attacking arm down past **B**'s right hip. **B** pivots back to center with this action, aligning themselves with **A**'s center line.

2. As **A** cuts to the right shoulder, **B** blocks **A**'s forearm with the back of their forearm. Once the block is made, the knife will hook over **A**'s wrist, while circling the arm clockwise and manipulating **A**'s attacking arm down past **B**'s left hip.

3. As **A** cuts to the left hip, **B** pivots right and extends the right arm forward and low, making connection with **A**'s forearm with the back of their forearm. Once the block is made, the knife will hook over **A**'s wrist, while circling the arm clockwise and manipulating **A**'s attacking arm up and over **B**'s head, past **B**'s right shoulder. **B** pivots back to center with this action, aligning themselves with **A**'s center line.

4. As **A** cuts to the right hip, **B** extends the right arm forward and low, making connection with **A**'s forearm with the back of their forearm. Once the block is made, the knife will hook around **A**'s wrist, while circling the arm counterclockwise and manipulating **A**'s attacking arm up and over **B**'s head, past **B**'s left shoulder. **B** pivots back to center with this action, aligning themselves with **A**'s center line.

Double Knives

Using two knives at the same time is a great way to create greater dynamics in a fighter. This is useful if you want one character to be more menacing or higher skilled. Having one fighter start off with two knives and the other unarmed is a great dynamic that can allow for a weapon takeaway, to where both fighters can end up with a weapon. An example of a fight like this would be the kitchen fight in The Raid 2. The main issue I have experienced when working with performers using two knives is that the dominant side performs better than the non-dominant side. To avoid these types of problems, it is always good to train all actions with both hands, as weak attacks can break the flow and believability of a scene. The trick to two-weapon fighting is keeping the flow and action moving. The following is a simple exercise to get both arms flowing in a cutting drill.

1. Right Hand Cut – Diagonal High to Low from the Right
2. Left Hand Cut – Diagonal High to Low from the Left
3. Right Hand Cut – Diagonal Low to High from the Right
4. Left Hand Cut – Diagonal Low to High from the Left
5. Right Hand Stab – Forehand Stab followed by a Horizontal Cut Right to Left
6. Left Hand Stab – Forehand Stab followed by a Horizontal Cut Left to Right
7. Right Hand Cut – Vertical Cut Down followed by a Forward Stab
8. Left Hand Cut – Vertical Cut Down followed by a Forward Stab

This exercise is just one quick example of double-knife work, as there are endless possibilities of combinations that can be created for drills or choreography.

Knife Throws

Knife throws are exciting and dynamic. From films like *John Wick 3: Parabellum*, *The Matrix*, *Mr. & Mrs. Smith*, and *The Hunger Games*, to plays and musicals such as *Wait Until Dark*, *Annie Get Your Gun*, and *The Pajama Game*, knife throws are used to create excitement, danger, or easy kills, but they work completely differently from film to stage.

In film, the effect can be created either by the use of editing, such as filming one actor throwing a knife or acting like they are throwing the knife, then filming the victim with the knife already in them and cutting between the two shots; or through the use of computer-generated imagery (CGI), such as in *John Wick 3: Parabellum*, where all the knives and axes being thrown are completely CGI.

In theatre, it is a different style all together. We have two basic options. The first is where the knife is being thrown into a person. Here, the victim will already be holding a knife, and when the actor pretends to throw the knife at them, they lift the knife quickly into place and react. The other option is if the knife is being thrown into an object. Here, the props department and your technical director become the stars of your action. I have found that I tend to use one of three methods for creating the effect of a knife being thrown: manual push, spring lever, and pneumatic/hydraulic.

The act of throwing the knife:

The first trick in throwing knives in theatre is **do not throw a knife in theatre**. Seriously, never throw an object- – especially a prop knife – at anyone or anything.

For the action of throwing the knife, the actor will hold the knife, usually in a fashion to where everyone in the audience can see it. For this example, let us put them downstage right. The actor will hold the knife in their right hand. They have two options for throwing – underhand or overhand.

If throwing underhand, the knife should be low and behind the actor; they can be holding it by the tip or the handle. They would then quickly lift their arm up in front of them and either roll the knife over in their hand, hiding it along their forearm, or allow the arm to arch over to their upstage left side and hide the knife either in their left hand or in a pocket.

If throwing overhand, they will lift the knife above their head in their downstage arm and, as before, swinging their arm forward, they will either roll the knife over in their hand, hiding it along their forearm, or allow the arm to arch over to their upstage left side and hide the knife either in their left hand or in a pocket.

The danger with rolling or flipping the knife in their hand is that the blade may come loose with too much force or if the performer's hand is slick. A trick that I have seen used is to drill a hole in the end of the knife the actor will be holding and fasten a bolt through the hole. A metal, plastic, or wooden disk with holes just a little larger than the bolt but smaller than the bolt head and nut can be inserted on both sides of the knife, with the bolt through them, which will allow for the knife to turn over in their hand without losing grip of the blade.

The act of the knife sticking in a wall:

Here is where the three methods I have used in the past come to play. I will start with the simplest and work my way towards the complex. For the sake of these examples, let us imagine that our performer is throwing the knife at a wall. The wall will have an opening for the knife covered by paper, thin rubber, or another material painted the same color as the wall with a slit cut in it that the audience cannot see.

The block slide: This is the simplest and cheapest of all the actions. Here, a knife will be attached to a block of wood, usually via a bolt drilled through the end of the knife. The block will be on a rail attached to the back of the wall, where it cannot be seen by the audience. A stagehand will stand back behind the wall and quickly push the knife through. The sound of the block hitting the wall will make the sound of the knife hitting.

The spring lever: This one takes a bit more work. First, you will need a spring hinge; you can find these at most hardware stores or online. Take the knife and cut off about half an inch from the tip. I recommend wielding the knife if it is metal, but I have also seen bolts and screws used, to the hinge. If using rubber or wood, make sure the hinge is not so strong that it will snap the wood or make the rubber wobble. For this, you will want your hole in the wall to be the size and length of the full knife (minus the cut tip), as it will drop down through the slit in the cover. The knife will be held in place by a pin or clamp, something that can be quickly released by a stagehand on cue. Note: You probably do not want to use this method if the knife has to be thrown at someone as a trick, such as in *The Pajama Game*, as the space needed for the knife to exit is fairly large compared to either of the two slide methods.

Pneumatic/hydraulic slide: Simple but more expensive. I have used this once in a show, and it worked perfectly. The only issue you may find is if the slide makes a sound. Here, like the block slide detailed earlier, the knife is attached to a slide rail system behind the wall. This is connected to either a pneumatic or hydraulic pump that pushes the knife through the opening in the wall quickly. This can be triggered remotely or at the slide by a stagehand.

Need to pop a balloon? No problem, just use either of the slide methods described previously and attach a pin or needle with glue or tape to the upstage side of the end of the handle, and as the knife exits, it will pop the balloon. You will not need to have very much of the pin or needle sticking out past the handle, as all it needs to do is make contact first with the balloon. Side note: This same thing can be done with darts, if you ever need to stage a carnival game.

Grip Changes and Hand Transfers

Sometimes a choreography will need a quick grip change or a little flair. In film, we see knife flips, hand transfers, and grip changes in many fights. And in film, these are easy because the performer can do multiple takes, but how can we bring that same level of flair to a live theatrical show? Practice. Flips, transfers, and changes can be done live, but they take practice to get right so that when the adrenaline kicks in, you can still perform them safely.

Performance Note: As you are learning the techniques in this section, you will want to keep your eyes on what you are doing. However, when you are in performance, you will want to keep your eyes on your partner and not on your own weapon. As you build up your skill in these actions, work them to where you can perform them without having to watch your weapon the whole time.

Grip Changes

There will be times when you will need to change from an overhand grip to an underhand grip, or vice versa, during choreography. This can be a little tricky, but with practice you can make it smooth and natural. Here are a few techniques for making the transition.

Pinch and Pivot

The pinch and pivot method is the safest grip change to perform, as you never let go of the knife during the transition.

Holding the knife blade up and in either a fist or saber grip, move your fingertips and thumb to the side of the handle. While applying pressure to your middle or ring finger and thumb, rotate the knife forward, allowing the bottom of the handle to pass inside your hand as the weight of the blade moves the knife. The blade will drop down as the handle inverts in your grip. Once the blade is down, reset your grip. A couple of things to keep in mind as you do this technique: If your knife has a long handle, you may need to choke down on the grip before pivoting. If your knife is single edged and you want your edge facing forward after the pivot, you may need to turn the knife in your hand.

To go from underhand to overhand grip is just a little trickier but uses the same technique. While applying pressure to your middle or ring finger and thumb, rotate the knife up, allowing the bottom of the handle to pass inside your hand as the weight of the blade moves the knife up. This may take one of two methods of momentum to perform the pivot. The first can be a simple lift of the hand, providing a pivoting swing to the knife. The second can be done by using the lower fingers under the pinch to push on the handle and help the blade forward and up into the overhand position.

The Finger Twirl

The finger twirl method of changing your grip works great with narrow-gripped knives and daggers, such as switchblades or stilettos. This method requires a bit more finger dexterity than any of the other grip changes, as the handle will be completely manipulated by your fingers. There are many ways to do a finger twirl; here I am breaking down the one I always use and teach. I use this method because it works with just about any size handle and after the twirl, there is not much need to reset the grip or chance of accidently putting the blade in my hand or fingers.

From an overhand grip, move your fingertips and thumb to the side of the handle. While applying pressure to your index and middle finger and thumb, tuck your ring finger and little finger inside on the same side as your thumb. Now, releasing the thumb, use your middle finger and ring finger to manipulate the pivot of the knife. The blade should move down on the inside of your hand, while the bottom of the handle moves up on the outside of your hand. As the pivot completes, allow your index finger to move around the handle to the same side as the ring and little finger. At this point, your index, ring, and little finger will be on one side of the handle while your middle finger is on the other. Your knife should now be facing down. Apply pressure with your thumb to the handle and slip your middle finger around the handle, to where you are now holding the knife properly in an underhand grip.

Do the exact same action to go from an underhand grip to an overhand grip.

The Flat Spin

With this change, and the ones to follow, you will be letting go of the knife in order to make the transition. These take a lot of practice to get right, and even more to do correctly during a performance.

For the flat spin, you will open your hand and with either the index or middle finger, slightly push on the knife handle while doing a small diagonal lift with the hand. Your hand will not actually be flat but at more of a 30-degree angle, with the thumb and index finger up, and you will follow that angle on the lift. The knife pivots on its handle in your palm as you quickly open and close your hand with the movement. This works in both overhand and underhand grips. You will probably drop the knife often when first learning this action. Be very aware of your feet and your surroundings.

The Flip

Not only are we letting go of the knife, but it will also now spin in the air. Take your time learning this one and do not attempt it on stage unless you are very comfortable with the action every time, as this is probably the easiest one to drop or miss of all the transitions. Again, be very aware of your feet and your surroundings.

For the flip, holding the knife in an overhand grip, hold your hand palm up and, using the fingers of your hand and a small flick of the wrist, flip the knife over. The knife will do a half turn in the air, with the blade of the knife moving backwards towards you and the handle moving forwards away from you. Grab the knife securely, and you should now be in an underhand grip. Do the same thing again, and you should be in an overhand grip. If you do a full spin, the knife will return into an overhand grip. As you get better at this action, you can add more lift to the knife, making it spin higher in the air.

The Release and Catch

With this technique, there is no spin or flip of the knife as you will be releasing the knife in the air and catching it in a different grip. The mistakes that often happen with beginners with this action is either missing the knife altogether or not getting hold of the knife and instead of grabbing it, the hand hits the handle, causing it to 'fly' away from the performer. So yet again, I advise you to be very aware of your feet and your surroundings.

To perform this action, hold your knife in an overhand grip and either turn your hand palm up or palm down; this will cause the blade to be flat in front of you, with the tip either pointing out to your right or in to your left. Lift your hand quickly and let go of the knife in front of you; try not to put a spin on the knife. As soon as you let go, pull your hand away and then reach out and grab the knife in the opposite manner in which you let go. For example, if you let go of the knife with your palm up, grab the knife with your palm down. Pay attention and grab only the handle. This will take you from an overhand grip to an underhand grip.

This can also be performed with the knife vertical; however, it requires you to turn your hand over, using more of your arm to twist by lifting the elbow for the catch to happen properly, whereas with the flat grab it is more of a forwards and backwards action, with a rotation of forearm and wrist only.

Hand Transfers

Another element you can add to your fight is switching hands during the choreography. And while you can just pass the knife from one hand to the other, why not add a little flair to the action? In this section, we are going to look at some knife transfers that add some energy and excitement to the fight. All these transfers are done by either tossing or dropping the knife between the hands. As with the flips and spins described earlier, be careful and take your time learning them. Cool moves only work when they are done correctly, and dropping a knife in the middle of a fight can ruin the moment.

The Horizontal Transfer

The horizontal transfer works much like tossing a ball between your hands. The trick to this action is to try not to put any rotation or flip on the knife, so that each hand catches the weapon with the edge forward. This transfer was used in the movie *Rebel Without a Cause*, and while Buzz (Corey Allen) is doing the transfer back and forth, Jim (James Dean) reaches out and knocks it out of the air, disarming Buzz.

The Vertical Transfer

Much like the horizontal transfer, this transfer moves vertically from high to low and vice versa. The first action is very easy; it is a high to low drop, letting the weight of the weapon carry it. The second action uses a little energy, as the lower hand tosses the weapon up to the receiving hand. Again, the trick here is not to put a rotation on the knife. This transfer was used in the movie *The Hunted*, during the final knife fight between L.T. (Tommy Lee Jones) and Aaron (Benicio del Toro). During a struggle where L.T. has Aaron in a lock, Aaron drops the knife down to his left hand and cuts across L.T.'s stomach.

The Drop Flip

In this action, we are taking the vertical drop transfer and adding a bit of flair to it. We can enhance this move by intentionally adding a flip to the action, so that it goes from an overhand grip in the upper hand to an underhand grip in the lower receiving hand. An action to pay attention to is to make sure the edge of the blade remains forward. Letting the blade drop first, then adding a small flick of energy to the handle of the knife, will create the flip. Too much energy, and it will over-rotate; not enough energy, and the blade will drop straight down.

The Side Flip

The side flip is a fun action to add for extra flair in a fight. Much like a juggler's throw, you will be transferring the knife from one hand to the other with a rotation. This can be a half rotation or full rotation depending on how you want to catch the knife. This move can also be done in either overhand or underhand starting position. The trick here is to add some height to the toss so that the knife has time to rotate. This will take much practice to get right, and even more to accomplish in the moment of performance. A good use of this flip is in the HBO series *Game of Thrones*, in the Arya and Brienne fight scene (S7 E4). Arya (Maisie Williams), having just been disarmed of her sword by Brienne (Gwendoline Christie), draws her knife in her right hand and does a full rotational flip to her left hand, then engages to threaten Brienne to end the fight.

The Flip Back

The flip back is just a variation on the side flip, where we go from having the knife in the forward hand to the knife in the back hand. Like before, this needs a little extra momentum and height, as you will be doing a full rotation in the air and catching the knife palm up in the opposite hand. Allow the lift energy of your forward hand's index finger to assist in the throw back. Be careful not to put too much energy into the throw, or you will just be throwing it into your chest.

Closing Comments

From basic actions to advanced flair, you should now have a solid understanding of the art of knife fighting for stage and screen. Like any skill, the more you practice, the better you will become and the more natural the movements will feel. Be aware that you can get away with more detailed work in film than you can in live theatre. In theatre, you must deal with uninterrupted action, actors' adrenaline, and audience sight lines, whereas in film, you can zoom in, frame each action perfectly, do takes, and repeat until you have the right shot.

10

FINAL THOUGHTS FOR ACTORS AND DIRECTORS

Developing a fight is more than just slapping some moves together. An analogy that was once told to me goes like this: "The moves are the raw ingredients of a great meal. It is about how you take them, prepare them, how they work together, and then finally how they are presented on a plate and served". Good choreography keeps everyone safe and serves the story; a superb and dynamic fight not only keeps everyone safe and serves the story but also builds the proper tension and excitement and draws a reaction from the audience.

In this final chapter of the book, we are going to explore some of the ideas and concepts that go into putting a finished fight together. In a perfect world, every theatre show – no matter where it is located or how small the show or budget is – would have a skilled fight director putting the action together, just as we wish every student or independent, low-budget film would have skilled stunt performers and a stunt coordinator. Unfortunately, that is not always the case, and we must move

DOI: 10.4324/9781003147862-10

forward – but we must move forward safely. I hope that is what this chapter can do for you; whether you are a performer or a director, I hope that the information contained in this final chapter helps you become a better, safer performer or director. Please remember that a book does not replace professional training or qualified fight direction.

So what is it that goes into making a fight dynamic? For those answers, we are going to examine what I call the five elements of a dynamic fight: Physical Actions, Emotional Actions, Reactions, Vocal Actions, and Lines of Sight. These elements work together to create an action sequence that will build tension, enhance the story, serve the characters, and keep the action safe and repeatable.

The Five Elements of Dynamic Fights

1. Physical Actions

    Every move the performer does is based on physical actions, but choreography is more than just moving the weapon around in a safe fashion. The actor must utilize their entire training and employ full-body acting. From breathing, to body mechanics, to footwork, to offhand techniques, to facial expressions, the entire body of the actor must be utilized in telling the story and engaged in the performance. All too often, the actor can get so focused on the weapon work that they forget to move their body to match the energy being put into the choreography. Full-body engagement keeps the story believable, and when these actions are developed at the beginning of the choreography training, they will be present at the performance. Like I stated at the beginning of the book, don't wait until the last minute to add these actions; make them part of the training and rehearsal process from the first day of rehearsal. As an actor, you must be aware of your total physicality while working on the actions. As a director, you need to remind your performers that a choreography is more than just the moves of the fight – it is all the actions, from facial expressions to movements, breathing, and fighting techniques.

    Keep the feet active. Footwork is the base from which the actor moves. If your feet have no active movement, then the choreography has no active movement. Footwork can be used even in the tightest of spaces to increase the dynamic actions of the body. Proper footwork also keeps the actor safe in body alignment and moving across the stage. A dynamic choreography will utilize the whole body. As an actor, you need to keep your feet engaged in the action, paying attention to your stage and your surroundings and staying in proper alignment with the moves. As a director, you need to make sure that the fight moves around without a sense of disjointed actions or danger from set pieces or other performers.

Add leans and avoidances. Not every action is going to land a hit, and that is a good thing. Narrowly escaping a move or using cunning to avoid an action builds the tension needed in a fight. If every action lands a hit, then it is either going to be a very quick fight, a very boring fight, or both. Move the body around and keep yourself active before, during, and after the action. Even if your character dies, the body is active after the hit, as you are the moving to the floor, or as the character is struggling for life while dying slowly on stage. As an actor, you need to pay attention to what your body is doing during the fight and the story it is telling. It is all too easy to want to be a badass fighter who never misses an action, but ask yourself if that is really serving the story your character needs to be telling. What level of energy should your character have in the moment? Directors need to beware the constantly bobbing performer. The physical energy needs to be directed into actions and not just nervous body energy. Remember, the moves must constantly support the character and the choreography. Fights should play out like a game of chess, where each fighter is testing the other while trying to find the finishing move. A dynamic choreography utilizes levels of actions both connecting and missing.

Be aware of what both arms are doing. It is very easy for an actor to be so focused on what the knife hand is doing that they completely forget what the offhand is doing. Keep the offhand active and ready, as it should be part of the story just as much as the feet and body. As an actor, you need to think about both arms, not just the weapon arm. Keeping the other arm up and active in front of you allows you to be ready for a block or counter action. It keeps your whole body active on stage. As a director, you need to sometimes remind your performers to stay active and engaged.

Keep the actions concise. Sometimes it is easy in theatre to want to make the actions too big, or to allow the energy of the choreography to grossly exaggerate movements. Although there may be times when we want that, such as in comedies or stylized actions, most of the time we want to keep the action believable and focused. As a performer, you will want to amplify the actions just enough so that the audience and your partner can keep up with the story, but if the actions are too exaggerated, the time it would take to set for the next action becomes disjointing and the 'danger to the character' aspect of the fight is lost. As a director, you will want to make sure that the actions fit the scene and the story. You are the outside eyes for the performers and will help guide their actions to fit your vision and utilize actions that move the story forward and keep the audience engaged.

Speed is your enemy. This is something you have read many times in this book, and I talked about at the start of the book. Take your time while learning the moves and the choreography. Once the moves are learned and you can perform the choreography all the way through with no mistakes, then you can start to speed the fight up to performance level. Your fight needs to move at the right pace. Too slow and it is boring; too fast and it looks unintentionally sloppy. As a performer, remember your tempo for the actions, as they will change throughout the choreography; do not rush yourself or your partner. Make each action clean and concise. As a director, focus on the rhythm of the choreography. Remember, the fight continues and enhances your vision and must remain a believable part of the world you have created. If the show is realistic or stylized, the fight must fit and that *dramatic convention* must be maintained.

Eyes help tell the story. Eye contact is important in the safety element of stage combat. When the actors are looking at each other, they are aware of their partner and working together. The eyes also help tell the emotional story of where the character is focused and their state of mind. As a performer, if your character is unskilled and scared, you may be watching the attacks of the aggressor. If your character is skilled, you will focus more on your opponent and their full-body actions. Even if you are playing a character who is scared, you will still need to keep checking in with your partner. This lets them know that you are still engaged in the choreography and are ready for the actions. As a director, pay attention to the performers' focus – does it match their characters and the emotional moment of the fight? Help guide them to establish focus when needed and keep the story being told.

Distance makes a difference. The space between the performers is just as important a part of the fight as the moves themselves. Advancing on what I discussed at the beginning of the book, the use of distance can greatly benefit or hamper a fight. If the actors are too close together, the audience cannot see the action; too far apart and the actions are unbelievable. As a performer, you need to be aware of your distance at all times. You will need to make adjustments and alterations throughout the actions to maintain proper distance. As a director, you will need to help guide the performers by letting them know when they are too close or too far away. Think of the story you are wanting the actors to tell and figure out how distance may be a part of that story.

2.   Emotional Actions

The emotional actions of a choreography are just as important as the physical actions. If our characters are not engaged in the fight emotionally, we are left with an empty feeling and have no attachment to the outcomes or consequences of the actions. Fights should always happen for a reason, and the consequences of the fight should be significant to the story and the characters; without the actors portraying those emotions to us, it will fall flat.

The more out of control the character, the more in control the actor. If a character is enraged to the point of physical violence, the actor must characterize that rage in a controlled and repeatable manner. As a performer, you must take care to maintain the choreography. Do not let the tempo of the actions or the rhythm of the fight change just because you are feeling your character's emotions or because your adrenaline is in full force during opening night. As a director, you will want to talk about the emotional elements in the choreography, walk through it, perform it slowly with full emotion, and repeat as much as needed to develop the proper actions. Let the actors use their skills as performers in creating the emotion of the scene but keep the actions under control for safety and story. Talk to your actors about what expressions need to be used and where the characters are focused. Explore which emotion(s) are driving the action forward. Why are the characters fighting? Is it revenge, anger, hate, frustration, fear, love, honor, self-preservation, or is the character showing off? Are they the ones instigating the actions or are they on the defensive? What is the emotion at the end of the fight? What are the consequences of winning or losing? How do the emotions change throughout the fight? It is important to have the performers and director talk about these questions before and during the work, as this will build a more dynamic choreography.

The emotions go beyond the actions. Very rarely does a fight just end. Even after the final action or killing blow, the emotion is still there. When Don José stabs Carmen, that is not the end of the emotion. In his rage and jealousy, he stabs her, and while Escamillo is applauded by the crowds offstage, Carmen dies. Don José kneels and, with all the previous emotions along with the heavy weight of guilt, sings "Ah! Carmen! ma Carmen adorée!". The scene continues, the emotions continue. Sometimes those emotions are put onto the audience to carry. When Juliet, finding Romeo dead, stabs herself, that loss of love and emotion is passed on to the audience to carry until the next person enters on stage and takes that emotion on themselves. Fights are very rarely a standalone action. As a performer, ask yourself what your character's emotions are and how they change during the fight. As the director, it is your job to help the performers and provide those moments at the end of the fight.

3. Reactions

You can have the greatest moves ever written in a choreography, but one wrong, bad, or missing reaction will halt the audience's connection almost immediately. Reactions keep your story moving forward. They also help keep the audience believing actions that are happening, even when they know it's a staged fight. The suspension of disbelief will be maintained or lost by the quality of reactions from each performer in the fight. These reactions also fall onto other characters who may be onstage or in frame during the scene.

Every action must have a reaction. This goes beyond the *action-reaction-action* technique of stage combat that I discussed in the opening chapter. Here we are talking about responses. The attack must be parried, blocked, avoided, or accepted. The emotional action of one character must have an emotional reaction from the other. Even the act of simply pulling out a knife must have a reaction from other actors on stage. If a character is injured, they must react appropriately, or inappropriately if it is a comedy. An example I love to use, and will later use when talking about vocal actions, is stubbing a toe. When you stub your toe, very rarely are you just going to look down and shrug your shoulders. We react physically by pulling our foot away from the offending object, and usually end up holding the poor injured toes. We bring the foot into us. Just like if you were to accidently prick your finger with a sewing needle or pin — you quickly pull your injured finger away, usually clutching the hand in a fist. In these instances, an object is making a connection with part of our body, and our body's reaction to the pain is to move away from the pain. So, too, must this be done in a choreography. As a performer, ask yourself if you are acting or reacting. As a director, help the performers find the reactions, emotional or physical, to the actions happening around them and to them.

Physical reactions must follow the flow of energy. Here, we are talking about the flow of energy between the two combatants. Imagine watching a fight and a character throws a right hook, hitting the other character on the left side of the face, and the actor reacts by turning their head to their left. The *flow of energy* is disrupted by the incongruity of the reaction; if you're hit on the left, you should turn to your right. Now, the audience may not immediately say to themselves, "Oh, the actor turned the wrong way", but they will have a mental disruption that will pull them from the fight. Another example where the reaction creates an undesired effect is if, when a character gets lightly slapped in the face, the actor receiving the action overreacts by turning out with a big action and falls to the ground. If the purpose of the actions were to create a comic effect, then well done; however, if it was meant to build dramatic tension, the actions and reactions failed. As a performer, if your character is cut across their forearm, they must react with the injured body part in a way that follows the natural flow of energy (see the section on reactions to cuts in Chapter 8). As a director, you need to keep watch and make sure that the flow of energy is in all the action and that the reactions match the story you are trying to tell.

The body is a solid object, not a stiff object. One area where inexperienced fight performers struggle is the separation of the physical actions of a reaction. An example of this is where a character is lightly hit in the face and instead of just the head turning, the whole body turns as one reaction. As previously stated, this could be used for good comedic moments, but when trying to create a believable choreography, it disrupts the actions. There are over 300 joints in the human body. The part of the body hit first, reacts first. Let me repeat that — the part of the body hit first, reacts first. If a character is stabbed or cut in the arm, that arm moves first, followed by the shoulder, the upper body, and then the other arm may come and hold/cover it. If a character is hit in the face, the head turns first, then the shoulders, then the back twists, then the hips, legs, and eventually the feet if the flow of energy requires it. If a character is avoiding a belly cut, the torso moves away from the object first, then the rest of the body follows. As a performer, you want to constantly be aware of your body movements and work to separate the physical actions. As a director, you will need to keep a keen eye on the physical movements of the performers and watch for any stiffness or lacking body reactions.

4. Vocal Actions

In the last of the actions category, we will examine the use of the voice in creating a dynamic fight. The voice gives us one of our 'musical' elements of a fight. In film, this can be done in post-production, but on stage it must be done live every time. Vocal actions fall both into the actions and reactions categories. They cover the range from energy and effort put forth to reactions to pain, reactions to emotions and, of course, the dialogue of the scene. Vocalizations can be voluntary, involuntary, cathartic, exasperated, startling, intimidating, or controlled with the action. Not only do these sounds help create the excitement of a fight, but they also work to keep the performers properly breathing during the choreography.

A sound to the action. Without knaps or underscoring, the only sounds we get in a knife fight are the sounds of the combatants. It is important that we strike a balance with the vocalization. Too much, and we sound like a Bruce Lee film; too little, and we get nothing from it. As a performer, find the moments where you can punctuate a move with a sound or can give vocalization to a block or avoidance. Try to find natural sounds early in the work, as what you rehearse is what you will perform. As a director, play with different sounds, volumes, and inflections while setting the choreography. Also, watch out for using "pow", "bang", or anything along those lines; as I stated before, if it is done during rehearsal, it will be done on stage.

If it cannot be seen, then it needs to be heard. Another great use of sound is as a vocal cue to your partner for an action happening that they cannot see. If you are performing an action behind your partner, a vocal cue, along with a touch cue, can allow them to react to the action. This also works if you are doing an action that the audience cannot see, such as a stab in the back with the victim facing the audience. As a performer, consider ways you can give vocal cues to your actions, both for your partner and for the audience. As director of the scene, make sure that both performers are giving a vocal cue when needed, and be the audience's ears for the volume of vocalization.

Pain hurts, so let's hear it. A cut, a stab, the final death blow — all of these deserve a good sound reaction. They let the audience know that something happened and lend a sense of realism to the fight. The level of severity of the injury, and the location, will alter the sound you make. Think of your sounds the same way you do in a hand-to-hand fight. The vocal scale of pain will match the action. Small cuts get a quicker, sharper sound, while stabs and deeper cuts have an exasperated, deeper sound. Your death blows, however, will have a more guttural, low sound that may be sustained with your breath longer. Using variance in sounds relating to pain help build variety and create the music of a fight. As a performer, think about the different sounds you can make, play with them, and find what feels natural as a reaction. Directors should pay attention to the level of pain and the sound being produced. Help your performers discover the right sounds.

5. Lines of Sight

Lines of sight are where the sleight of hand and stage magic happen. The audience will believe what they cannot see. Utilizing the lines of sight allows the viewer to think actions are happening much closer in proximity than they are physically. This allows us to keep the actors safe while at the same time creating a dynamic and exciting fight. Understanding staging, the type of stage you are on, and where the audience is in relation to the action are factors that must be considered at every step of the choreography. Think of the fight as a game of show and tell. Some moves we will show to the audience; others we will tell with reactions as we hide the actual action. Next we will examine the different ways we can manipulate these lines of sight.

Upstage/downstage. The use of rotation in a fight will not only help in creating dynamic movement but also help in the selling of actions such as body cuts, quick thrusts, or other actions you do not wish the audience to see, especially regarding how far away the actual action is from the performer's body. This use of action is great for when the show is in a proscenium theatre style or the audience only has one perspective on the fight.

In the round, move around. Performing fights in a space where the audience fully surrounds or mostly surrounds the stage can be tricky — spaces like thrust, black boxes, or arena-style theatres. Here, the fight must move around and can add rotations during an action to hide the gap between actors. This does not mean that the fight must constantly circle around, as that would get very boring and repetitious to watch. However, using circular passes or rotations at key moments in the choreography will help sell (and hide) the action. As performers, review your footwork and look for ways in which you can smooth the rotation of your actions. Directors can help by putting in offline attacks or avoidances that help move the fight.

5a. Use of Implied Violence

I must admit, this is my favorite kind of violence. Implied violence is where the action happens out of view from the audience. The audience's mind will imagine far worse than I can ever stage. A fight can move behind an object like a couch, and one actor can fall down as the other actor − from the audience's point of view − stabs them repeatedly. This is a great way of creating a high amount of violence without having to show it. This also presents us with a way to stage violence without having to use blood effects. Now there may be times when you want the audience to fully see and experience the violence, such as in *Sweeney Todd: The Demon Barber of Fleet Street* or the opening of the opera *Dead Man Walking*, but this is a great alternative to presenting violence that the audience cannot see, or you may be in a setting in which that level of violence isn't needed to be seen. Another method of creating implied violence is having the actors fight their way offstage or behind a large set piece, with only one actor returning − and depending on their time offstage, they can reenter covered in blood (think of Macbeth's death). As a performer, you must still perform with the same intensity and emotion with implied violence as you would with anything the audience can see. As a director, this is a great way to create violence in a way that can tell the story without fully showing the actions. There are many ways to use implied violence, and I highly recommend utilizing it any chance you get, as it is just another tool in your box.

There are many components that actors and directors can use to create an exciting and dynamic story on stage or in film, and these are just my personal five recommendations for actors and directors. There are many great books on acting, action directing, fighting on film, and the art of fight directing and choreography. Never limit yourself to just one person's knowledge or point of view. I have created a list of highly recommended books in Appendix C that I hope you will check out.

Bruce Lee once said, "Adapt what is useful, reject what is useless, and add what is specifically your own", and I love that. Because in that quote, he talks about developing your own martial arts style, and the same can be said about creating your unique theatrical combat style.

Be Safe, Be Dynamic, Be Entertaining.

GLOSSARY

Action(s) a.) Signifies an operation in its entirety, whether offensive or defensive. b.) Simple, compound, progressive, or combined movements of the knife and/or body used to accomplish the combatant's objectives within a fight.

Active Block A defensive action that deflects or redirects the energy of the attack.

Active Hand The non-weapon-bearing hand used to *block, check, lock, parry, strike* or *trap* the opposing weapon or parts of a partner's body, being kept active at chest level and not hanging at the side of the body. Also known as *Alive Hand*.

Active Footwork Footwork used to create dynamics within a fight.

Active Movement Any movement executed in an augmented, more vibrant fashion.

Adjustment Step a.) A small step intended to correct or realign the feet. b.) Any step that is not part of the choreography and is performed to fix a problem with distance or angle.

Advance The leading foot steps forward, followed by the trailing foot, ending in the same distance between the feet as in the on-guard position (without crossing them). The opposite of *Retreat*.

Aggressor   See *Attacker*.

Arm Bar   A lock that hyperflexes or hyper-rotates the elbow joint.

Arm Block   A defensive action made with the hand or arm, intended to stop a cut or thrust. A block can be made on either side of the body and in all lines.

Attack   a.) A simple or compound offensive action intended to harm one's opponent.

Attacker   (also Aggressor, Operator) The actor/combatant who sets upon, attacks, or assails another; the one executing the violent action. The initiator of an offense action.

Avoidance   A defensive movement of the body.

Back   a.) The "back" or false edge of a blade. b.) The rear or dorsal part of the human body. Generally used in reference to the rear portion of the upper torso. c.) To go, or cause to go, backward or in reverse.

Back Edge   See *False Edge*.

Backhand   The back of the hand.

Backpedal   To travel or move backward from an opponent through passing steps, or consecutive retreats, yet still facing them.

Belly Swipe   An exaggerated cutting action, giving the impression that it is targeting the belly.

Bind   A checking action made on the opponent's hand, arm, or leg, executed by blocking the attack and then moving it diagonally to the opposite quadrant (i.e., from the inside high to the outside low, or outside high to inside low, etc.).

Blade   The flat cutting edge of a knife or other tool or weapon.

Blade Flat   Also known as the Cheek or Face of a blade, refers to the widest flat sides of the blade.

Blade Point /Tip   The intersection of the front (edge) and back of the blade, intended for penetration or detailed cutting, very blunt on blades like the spey and very pointed on a blade like the clip point or stiletto.

Block   A physical defensive action made with the body or weapon that hinders, checks, neutralizes, or nullifies an opponent's attack to stop it from reaching its intended target.

Blunt   (also rebated) a.) A bladed weapon without a sharp edge. b.) A practice weapon. c.) Adjective – not sharp.

Boundary   Guideline that indicates or fixes a limit or extent to which an actor is willing to participate and establishes how others can behave around them and interact with them.

Butt   The bottom end of the handle on a knife.

"C" Grip   also known as a clamp grip or claw grip. This is where the aggressor creates a "C" with their hand, fingers together and thumb open out.

Cadence   The rhythm in which a sequence of movements is made.

Casting   Directing the energy past your partner to prevent force going into them.

Center Line   The center of the body. Two imaginary lines that bisect the body into equal halves, both vertical and horizontal.

Cheat/Cheat in/Cheat out   To 'cheat' is to turn your face or entire body either out to the audience (or camera) to be seen better without completely turning (so it still looks natural, but you are not completely in profile) or to face in to conceal something.

Check   The process of curbing or restraining the offending hand, arm, or leg after a successful block. The defending hand or arm remains in contact with the opponent's limb in order to sense their movements, feel or control the placement of the offending limb, and use that to both offensive and defensive advantage. These actions command the opposing hand or arm and may retain it or remove it with the action of an expulsion.

Close   a.) The action of stepping inside measure, usually into an offensive action, to gain tactical advantage for both defensive and offensive actions. b.) To cover or shut a line of engagement against an attack. c.) To bring your feet together.

Closed Line   A line of engagement where the defender's weapon or other defensive object prevents an attack to that line of engagement or targeting.

Communication   The ability to communicate with a partner while staying in character, with theatrical believability, and complete the set choreography.

Complex/Compound Footwork   An element of footwork that involves the execution of more than one simple component to complete the action.

Counter   An act of prevention of an attack or move made by your opponent.

Counterattack   An attack made into an attack, either cut or thrust, which is intended to hit the opponent before the final movement of the opponent's attack is executed.

Cross Block   A defensive action executed by bringing the hand or arm across the body (rather than up/down or to the outside of the body). Used to stop or deflect an oncoming attack.

Cross Step   An avoidance where the working leg crosses in front of the supporting leg (which stays in place or pivots on the ball of the foot), removing the combatant from the line of attack. A step that takes the body diagonally offline to either the right or left, ending with the legs crossed.

Cross Over   (Forward and Back): A two-part movement consisting of two steps forward (or backward) in which the hips remain facing in the same direction on both parts of the move.

Cue   An action said or done that provides a signal to a partner.

Cut   A stroke, blow, or attack made with the edge of a blade.

Cut Across the Head   A horizontal cut designed to look as if it will strike the head if it lands. It may travel right to left or vice versa and is usually avoided by ducking. Also called a "horizontal slash" to the head.

Cut Across the Stomach   A horizontal cut designed to look as if it would cut the stomach open if it landed. It may travel right to left or vice versa. The wrist is most often held to present the true edge and (for additional safety) the wrist/hilt lead with the butt of the weapon until the partner moves, at which point the cutting action is executed after it has passed the plane of the body. It is usually avoided by jumping back. Also called a "horizontal slash".

Cut to the Feet   A horizontal cut designed to appear to cut at the lower legs or feet, avoided by jumping up to create the illusion of jumping "over" the attacking blade. The tip of the attacking blade is usually directed to a spot on the floor a few inches in front of the defender's feet.

Defensive Guard   A stance where the non-dominant foot is forward.

Deflection   To cause something to change direction by interposing something; to turn aside from a straight course.

Diagonal Cut or Slash With Avoidance   An offline cut to either the inside or outside line. It may be a rising or a falling cut. It is usually avoided by leaning to the side away from the cut, with or without footwork.

Direct An attack or riposte made in the line of engagement.

Disarm The act of removing the partner's weapon by taking away a weapon or forcing the opponent to drop the weapon.

Distance The proper measure between two or more performers to safely execute techniques in theatrical combat.

Dominant The stronger or more controlled side. When right-handed, this is the right side; when left-handed, this is the left side.

Downstage The front of a stage, or the closest part of a stage to the audience.

Duck The vertical lowering of the body for the purpose of avoiding a cutting or a slashing action.

Edge The cutting surface of a blade that extends from point to heel.

Edge In The edge of the knife facing in towards you.

Edge Out The edge of the knife facing away from you.

Emotional Actions The representation of emotions created by the performer.

Envelopment A checking action made on the opponent's hand or arm, executed by blocking the attack and then by describing a circle with both arms in contact, bringing the opponent's arm back to the placement where the check began.

Evasion To avoid or escape an attack by moving the targeted area away.

Exaggerated Step A step larger than your normal stepping distance.

Expulsion (also Throw Off) Using the energy and movement of a check to throw or fling the opposing arm aside.

Extension The position or action during which a combatant reaches out with the limb, and if applicable, body and/or weapon, towards one's target.

Extended Parry A parry made with the arm in full extension.

Eye Contact The means of two performers looking in each other's eyes to assure mutual awareness and readiness to perform the techniques.

Fall Safely descending with the illusion of being out of control.

False Edge a.) A grind on the top of the blade, usually to allow a finer tip for better penetration. It can be very short or very long. b.) The edge of the blade opposite of the true edge on double-edged knives.

Feint Attack An attacking action made without intending to hit and designed to either probe the opponent's defensive reaction or to draw a reaction or a parry.

Fight Dynamics   Energy of movement, expressing intensity, accent, and quality.

Flank   Area of the body between mid-chest and the waist.

Flip/Throw   An offensive movement which controls or appears to control the victim's center, giving the illusion of lifting them off their feet and returning them to the ground – usually into a break fall or roll.

Flow of Energy   The direction in which effort is exerted through the body and through space.

Follow Through   Commitment to an action from beginning to end. To continue the cut or stab after the target has been struck, to the full extent of the blow.

Footwork   Activity or movement done with the feet.

Force   a.) The strength or energy as an attribute of physical action or movement. b.) To make someone do something against their will.

Fore Edge   *See True Edge.*

Forearm Block   One of the most common defensive actions for stopping a cut or stabbing attack. It is made with either the hard edges of bone or the muscle groupings on the back or inside of the forearm.

Forearm-Push   The use of the forearm to remove an object from your opponent's grip.

Forehand   a.) The palm of the hand. b.) The term used to indicate an attack, usually with the edge, delivered from the right.

Fore-Cut   A cutting attack with the fore or true edge of the blade.

Grab   A holding, clasping, or seizure of any part of the opponent's body/clothing/weapon with the hand(s).

Grapple   To engage in close quarters, fighting or struggling; to seize or hold.

Grasp   See *Hold.*

Grazing Strike   A hit with a body part or weapon that has the illusion of making contact, and then following through its target.

Grip   a.) The part of the handle normally held by the hand. b.) The manner in which the weapon is held.

Grounding   Having a stable base from which to perform fight choreography.

Guard   a.) The portion of the hilt between the blade and the grip that protects the hand. b.) A posture of defense.

Half Pass   A simple form of footwork that carries the foot forward or backward in the same manner as a pass, only bringing the foot to rest next to the opposing foot rather than one foot length past it.

Half Pronation/Supination (also Middle or Vertical Position) The placement of the weapon-bearing hand where the thumb is held at roughly 12 o'clock (Half Pronation) or six o'clock (Half Supination).

Half Step An action of footwork where the foot moves half the distance of your natural walking step.

Hammer Grip (also *Fist Grip*) The most basic of all grips, achieved by grabbing the handle of the weapon, wrapping your fingers around the grip, and allowing the thumb to wrap over the index finger.

Hand Grips to grasp or clasp/a firm hold with the hand.

Handle The handle of a knife is the portion you grip.

Head Swipe An exaggerated cutting action, giving the impression that it is targeting the head.

Heel Refers to the section of the blade next to the guard or handle.

High Lines The areas of the body above the waist.

Hit An offensive action which lands with point or edge on the target. An attack that successfully lands, or appears to land, with point or edge on the target.

Hold (also *Grasp*) To use one or both hands for clutching or grasping the opponent.

"Hook" Hand Also known as a "Cup" hand. Here the aggressor creates a hook with their hand, fingers together and curved, with the thumb flat against the side of the hand.

Horizontal Attack Any cutting attack that travels in a plane parallel to the floor.

Hunch The physical act of raising one's shoulders towards the head and bending the top of the body forward.

Hyperextend To go beyond the natural range of motion for a joint or part of the body moving about a joint. To extend in the sense opposite to flex, so as to attain an abnormally great angle.

Ice Pick Grip An underarm reverse grip with the hand grabbing the handle of the weapon, tip facing down, wrapping your fingers around the grip and allowing the thumb to wrap over pommel or butt of the weapon, to keep the knife/dagger from slipping through your hand.

Implied Violence Violence that is not seen by the audience and is only suggested or implied by the actor's physical actions viewable or heard by the audience.

In and Out Stab   A quick thrust with an object that is removed as soon as it enters.

In Distance   The measure where combatants could make contact with their partner by extending their weapon.

In Fighting   a.) When two combatants have closed distance and are inside normal measure. b.) The practice of moving inside fighting measure, getting up close to one's opponent to deliver a blow with the hand or hilt of a weapon. c.) Fighting at close quarters, hand to hand.

In Line   See *On Line.*

Indirect   An attack or riposte made in another line. An attack not delivered in the line of engagement.

Inside Block   A block used to deflect straight or circular strikes directed at the head or midsection. The forearm follows an inward path across your body and deflects the blow to the side.

Inside Line   a.) The area of attack and defense on a combatant, delineated by their vertical center line, which is furthest from their weapon-bearing side. Opposite of *Outside Line*. b.) The lines or parry positions protecting the side of the body farthest from the sword-arm.

Isolation   The ability to move or maneuver a specific part or parts of the body independent of the others.

Joint Lock   A grasp or hold that hyperflexes or hyper-rotates a joint, executed with one or both hands, applied to the joints in the wrist, arm, leg, etc., to immobilize one's opponent or to be used as a lever for further techniques such as a throw. See *Lock*.

Jump   A footwork action, either forward, backward, or up, where both feet leave the ground simultaneously.

Knee Attack   Any attack giving the illusion of contact with the knee.

Knee-Smash   The simulated action of using the knee to strike your partner's forearm, causing them to release whatever they are holding.

Knife   An offensive and defensive weapon or tool consisting of a blade with a sharpened longitudinal edge fixed in the handle, either rigidly or with a joint, or clap-knife. The blade is generally made of steel.

Lag/Back   The part of the body that is behind the others.

Lag Foot   See *Trailing Foot.*

Lead/Front   The part of the body that is ahead of the others.

Left Dominant   To have more control in, or to be more dexterous, with the left hand.

Lines of Attack or Defense   Referring to the imaginary planes that bisect the body into four equal sections, one vertical (delineating Inside and Outside) and one horizontal (delineating High and Low). The line may be open or closed, according to the relationship of the attacking blade, the target, and the defending blade.

Line of Engagement   The line between fighters, in which the weapons and their bodies are aligned and threatening.

Lines of Sight   The lines along which an audience or viewers see the action.

Linear Footwork   The practice of moving or working actions of the feet in straight lines rather than in circular planes.

Lock   A grasp or hold executed with a weapon or one or both hands, applied to the joints in the wrist, arm, etc., to immobilize one's opponent or to be used as a lever for further techniques such as a throw.

Masking   The action of 'hiding' combat techniques from the audience, to create the illusion of realism.

Measure   The distance between combatants when on guard, determined by the length or reach of the fighters.

Meter   A systematically arranged and measured rhythm for movement.

Micro Step   An action of footwork where your foot moves forward or backward only a few inches.

Mounted Position   A dominant ground grappling position, where one combatant sits, one leg on each side of the partner's torso, torsos facing each other.

Naked   An unsheathed blade.

Navaja   The navaja is a traditional Spanish folding-blade fighting and utility knife.

Neutral   The position where the hand is vertical with the thumb on top, i.e., halfway between supination and pronation.

Neutral Position   The neutral position is the bodily posture in which a performer is standing with the feet slightly apart and under the hips and shoulders with neither foot in the lead. The arms are hanging relaxed to each side of the body and the thumbs point forward.

Non-Dominant   The weaker or less controlled side. Opposite of dominant. When right-handed, this is the left side; when left-handed, this is the right side.

Object-Smash The simulated action of using an object to strike your partner or controlling your partner to strike an object.

Off/Open/Check-Hand The non-weapon bearing hand.

Off Line (also *Offline*) a.) Any attack that is directed to a target away from the body. b.) The relationship of combatants' bodies when the center lines of the combatants are offset. (Off Target) c.) Any action consisting of taking the body or weapon off the line of engagement.

Off Line Step Any movement that takes the body away from the Line of Engagement.

Off-Set (also Offset) Where the center lines of two combatants facing one another do not line up. One combatant is cheated to one side or the other. See also *Off Line*.

On-Guard The ready position from which a person can launch an offensive or defensive movement.

On Line (also *Online*) a.) A mode of theatrical fighting where attacks are aimed at specific body targets on the combatant. b.) The position of the two partners' bodies where the shoulders are precisely lined up, no matter where they are on stage. c.) Any action consisting of keeping the body or weapon on the line of engagement.

On Line Attack (also On Target) a.) An attack made directly to a target area of the body.

Open a.) The area on one's opponent that is unprotected. b.) An action to increase distance between combatants, or to move your feet apart.

Opening An unguarded area.

Out of Distance The measure where combatants cannot make contact with their partner by extending their weapon.

Outside Block a.) A block made on the outside or backside of the attacking hand, arm, or leg. b.) A defensive action made on the same side of the body, generally made on the outside or backside of the defending hand or arm.

Outside Lines The parts of the target on the side nearest to the knife arm. The parts of the body to the dominant side (right of the knife hand when one is right-handed, and left of the knife hand if one is left-handed).

Overarm The tip of the weapon facing up above the thumb when held.

Overhand Grip Holding a knife or dagger with the point above the hand. Opposite of *Underhand Grip*.

Partner   For the purposes of staged combat, all techniques both in attack and defense are worked in partnership, not in competition with a fellow actor.

Partnering   A process in which two or more combatants actively work together to safely and effectively make nonviolent actions appear real and dangerous.

Pass Backward   A linear step backward made by passing the lead foot to the rear. Opposite of the *Pass Forward*.

Pass Forward   The trailing foot crosses the leading foot to the fore one full step. Hips may or may not retain original orientation. Opposite of the *Pass Backward*.

Pass Through   To move an object through the targeted zone.

Passing Step/Crossover Step   Simple action of footwork that moves a combatant forward or backward by passing their lead foot to the rear beyond their lag foot into a new lag position, or by passing their lag foot to the front beyond their lead foot into a new lead position.

Phrase   A section of fight choreography. An exchange of blade patterns and body. movements that often ends with a choreographed punctuated pause (e.g., end in a corps a corps, a wound or kill, a break in the action, etc.).

Physical Actions   The actions created with the body by the performer.

Pivot   The act of swinging or turning the body while keeping the center of gravity fixed at a central point.

Pommel   A conical piece of metal located at the rear of the grip, which serves the dual purpose of locking the different parts of the weapon together and acting as a counterweight to the blade.

Pommel Attack   Any aggressive or offensive action, usually in close distance, delivered with the pommel of a weapon.

Pronation   The position of the hand where the palm is turned down.

Prop Knife   A blunted knife or dagger specifically designed for theatrical use. These can be wood, plastic, rubber, aluminum, or steel.

Reaction   An action performed or a feeling experienced in response to a situation or event.

Ready Stance   A relaxed stance from which offensive and defensive actions can instantly and equally be made.

Rear Foot   See *Lag Foot*.

Recover   Return to a guard position.

Redirection   An action where the hand or arm intercepts the attack and then immediately displaces or removes the threat by controlling the energy away.

Replacement Block   A block that uses both hands/arms, one after the other, to deflect and control the offending hand, arm, or leg. One hand begins the block; the other hand is then used to complete the block, 'checking' the offending limb and freeing the first hand for a counterattack.

Rest   A noticeable pause in action or movement.

Retreat   An action in the footwork that carries the body backward by moving the rear foot first and then the lead foot (without crossing them). Opposite of *Advance*.

Reverse Grip   a.) An underarm Hammer or Fist Grip achieved by grabbing the handle of the weapon, tip facing down, wrapping your fingers around the grip and allowing the thumb to wrap over the index finger. b.) An underhand grip on a weapon.

Rhythm   a.) The visible and audible variables of rate within beats and phrases of a fight. b.) The temporal pattern produced by the grouping and balance, or imbalance and unpredictability, of sounds and dialogue during a fight. The strong and weak elements in the flow of sound and silence.

Right Dominant   a.) Having the right hand and/or foot forward in an on-guard or ready stance. Generally referring to the lead foot in the on-guard stance. b.) To have more control in, or to be more dexterous with, the right hand.

Rip   (also *Gash*) a.) A violent attack made with the edge of the blade after the knife has penetrated the body with a successful thrust or stab. Once the blade is in the body, the edge is forcefully pulled through the flesh, tearing open the body and creating a deep laceration. b.) To cut or tear open. A wound to the body made with the edge of a bladed weapon that is more violent and damaging than a down cut. c.) To shred or tear fabric or paper.

Rising Block   a.) A block delivered upward to defend against a descending diagonal or vertical attack. b.) A deflection block, made with either arm, which protects the head.

Rocking   a.) The back-and-forth movement of the body during the execution of stationary footwork. b.) In active footwork, a partial advance or retreat (traveling about half the distance of a standard footwork) on the part of the combatants.

Rotation   The act of turning or rotating a limb (wrist, hand, head, arm, leg, etc.), the body, a weapon, or other object, in one direction or another. To turn circle-wise.

Saber Grip   (also Philippine Grip) An overarm grip. The hand is wrapped around the knife handle, while the thumb is placed on the top of either the handle or the spine of the blade.

Self-Inflicted   An injury or other harm done to oneself by oneself.

Seppuku   (also known as *hara-kiri*) Ritualistic suicide by disembowelment. Hara-kiri refers to the action of cutting the stomach, while *seppuku* represents the ritual and the traditional procedure of cutting the stomach.

Sharp   To have a keen edge or point; being well suited for cutting or piercing; a blade tapered to a fine edge or point; opposite of *blunt*.

Sheath   The case, covering, home, or lodging for the blade of a weapon when not in use; usually close fitting and conforming to the shape of the blade, the blade is generally thrust into the sheath by way of an opening at its top.

Shoulder Lock   An arm lock that hyperflexes or hyper-rotates the shoulder joint.

Shove   A strong or violent thrust or push with the feet, hands, or body, quickly moving a body away from the agent.

Side Grip   (also Modified Saber Grip) An overarm grip. The hand is wrapped around the knife handle, with the thumb wedged against the flat dimension of the blade.

Sidestep Evasion   Evasive actions that remove the body from the cutting plane of a diagonal or vertical swipe by lunging either to the left or to the right and leaning the torso into the lunge, creating, with the body, a parallel plane to the attack outside the cutting plane.

Simple Footwork   A basic element of footwork that involves the execution of one component.

Slit   To cut.

Small Step   An advance or retreat that is more a shuffle than a proper step.

Spatial Awareness   The state of being aware of your surroundings and your position relative to them.

Speed   The velocity or rate at which a fight is moving. The degree of quickness of movement, both of weapon and body, usually as a result of exertion, clarity, swiftness; also, the power of rate of progress.

Stab   a.) To drive, plunge, thrust, or kill with the point of a weapon. b.) To make or offer a thrust with the point of a weapon. c.) An attack made with the point of the knife delivered from a reverse or underhand position.

Stab and Stay   A thrust with an object that is left in position and is not removed.

Stance   The specific positioning of the feet and body as part of correct physical placement for a particular technique or form of combat.

Static Block   A defensive action that stops an attack. The defender's action is held in place, and the movement of the action comes to a complete stop.

Step   An action of footwork where the foot moves a normal distance, measured by the stride of your natural walk.

Straight Arm Parry   A parry executed with a straight or locked arm.

Straight Attack   An attack executed from an open guard position directly towards an opponent without changing the line of engagement.

Style   a.) A personal or characteristic manner of executing a fight. b.) An aesthetic and creative choice based on the actual mechanics of the weapon or form of combat.

Supination   The position of the hand when the palm is turned up.

Swipe   An exaggerated cutting action.

Takes   In film or television, a scene or sequence of sound or vision photographed or recorded continuously at one time.

Takeaway   To remove an object from the hand or opponent.

Target   The part of the body towards which an attack is directed.

Technique   A term for a specific move or action; especially in martial arts.

Tempo   The pace or speed at which an action happens.

Thrust   An attack made with the point of the weapon.

Thumbing the Edge   The act of placing the thumb against the fake edge of a knife to prevent the metal blade from touching the other actor's skin.

Thwart   A step that takes the body diagonally offline to either the right or left, ending with the legs open.

Timing   a.) The synchronization of each action and its corresponding reaction throughout a fight, the coordination of which incorporates both the speed at which actions are performed and the action–reaction speed of intrinsic partnered movements. b.) To acknowledge an opportunity or opening and execute the correct action at the best possible moment.

Training Knife   Any knife designed for use as a training aid. The blades are blunt, usually of aluminum, rubber, or synthetic resin, with rounded and blunted tips.

Transfer Block   See *Replacement Block*.

Transport   A checking action made on the opponent's hand, arm, or leg, executed by blocking the attack and then moving it vertically from a high line to a low line, or vice versa, but on the same side as the block took place.

Trap   An act or action that immobilizes an opponent's limb(s) and/or weapon to affect an attack or disarm.

Traverse   Any foot movement that takes the combatant offline.

True Edge   The edge of the double-edged blade that is aligned with the middle knuckles (the joint between the proximal and intermediate phalanges) of the hand holding it. On single-edge blades, it is the only edge.

Turn-out   The rotation of the leg at the hips which causes the feet (and knees) to turn outward, away from the front of the body. This rotation allows for greater extension of the leg, especially when raising it to the side and rear.

Turn-in   The rotation of the leg at the hips which causes the feet (and knees) to turn inward, towards the front of the body.

Unarmed   Without weapons.

Underarm   The tip of the weapon facing down below the little finger when held.

Underhand Grip   (also *Ice Pick Grip* and *Reverse Grip*) A way of holding a dagger or knife with the blade held beneath the hand (gripped with the thumb at the pommel) and managed as a stabbing weapon. Opposite of *Overhand Grip*.

Upstage The back of the acting area, or the furthest part of the stage away from the audience.

Upward Block Any one of numerous blocks used to neutralize an opponent's high line attack.

Vertical Attack Any cutting attack that travels from a high line to a low line, or vice versa, in a plane that is perpendicular to the floor.

Victim Control In theatrical combat, the actions of the choreography are controlled by the 'victim' (the one who is having the violence acted upon them).

Victim (also Recipient) The actor/combatant on the receiving end of any given attack. The recipient of an offensive action.

Violence The exercise of physical force (whether intentional or unintentional, armed or unarmed) so as to inflict injury on, or cause damage to, persons or property; or forcibly interfering with personal freedom.

Violent a.) Having some quality or qualities in such a degree as to produce a very marked or powerful effect (especially in the way of injury or discomfort). b.) Intense, vehement, very strong, or severe.

Vocal Cue In theatrical combat, a sound used to notify a scene partner of an upcoming or imminent action.

Vocal Reaction A sound preformed in reaction to an action delivered to or from a performer.

Walk-Through A slow rehearsal speed/pace.

Wield To use with the hand, to manage weapons.

Wring A twisting and squeezing action.

Wrist Lock A hold whereby one is controlled and immobilized by the wrist.

Weapon-Bearing Side The side of the body that brandishes or carries the weapon.

Yield a.) To give up or surrender; the action of giving in; submission. b.) To deliver, to render, to give up, to surrender. c.) To give way, to succumb.

APPENDIX A
ORGANIZATIONS

Academy of Performance Combat (APC)/theapc.org.uk
Academy of Dramatic Combat/academyofdramaticcombat.com
Academy of Theatrical Combat/theatricalcombat.com
Actors' Equity Association (AEA)/actorsequity.org
American Entertainment Armouries Association (AEAA)
American Guild of Musical Artists (AGMA)/musicalartists.org
Art of Combat International/artofcombat.org
British Academy of Dramatic Combat (BADC)/badc.org.uk
British Academy of Stage and Screen Combat (BASSC)/bassc.org
Fight Directors Canada (FDC)/fdc.ca
FightRight (Northern Ireland)/fightright.org.uk
Humble Warrior Movement Arts/humblewarriormovement.com
International Alliance of Theatrical Stage Employees, Moving Picture
    Technicians, Artists and Allied Crafts of the United States (IATSE)/
    iatse.net
Intimacy Coordinators Canada/intimacycoordinatorscanada.com
Intimacy Directors & Coordinators (IDC)/idcprofessionals.com

Intimacy Professionals Association (IPA)/intimacyprofessionalsassociation.com

Moving Body Arts (UK & EU)/movingbodyarts.com

Nordic Stage Fight Society/nordicstagefight.com

Rapier Wit/rapierwit.com

RC-Annie Ltd./rc-annie.com

Screen Actors Guild and the American Federation of Television and Radio Artists (SAG-AFTRA)/sagaftra.org

Society of American Fight Directors (SAFD)/safd.org

Society of Australian Fight Directors Inc. (SAFDI)/safdi.org.au

Stage Directors and Choreographers Society (SDC)/sdcweb.org

Theatrical Intimacy Education (TIE)/theatricalintimacyed.com

APPENDIX B
WEAPON SUPPLIERS

Baltimore Knife and Sword Co./baltimoreknife.com (a good rental house)

CAS Iberia/casiberia.com (a nice selection)

Century Martial Arts/centurymartialarts.com (good source for martial arts supplies)

Cold Steel/coldsteel.com (great quality knives, wonderful synthetic weapons)

Creations (formally known as Starfire Swords)/starfireswords.com (the weapon of the Renaissance Faire world)

Cuchilleria Albacete/cuchilleriaalbacete.com (great source for true navajas)

Fight Designer LLC/fightdesigner.com (a personal friend, a good selection of knives, but an amazing selection of firearms is the forte of this house)

Forte Stage Combat/fortecombat.com (a good rental house)

Keen Edge Knives/keenedgeknives.com (training, prop, and specialty knives and daggers)

Macdonald Armouries/macdonaldarms.com (custom weapons from an amazing artist and historian)

Museum Replicas Limited/museumreplicas.com (a decent selection)

Preferred Arms/preferredarms.com (rental house for film and theatre)

Purpleheart Armory/woodenswords.com (great Texas-owned business, lots of options)

RC-Annie/rc-annie.com (good friends, great supply for the UK and EU)

Rogue Steel/roguesteel.com (custom, rental, repairs, with a good selection)

Street Forge Armory/bit.ly/streetforgearmoury (great owners and creators, especially of African weapons; contact the owners for custom work, all their work is high quality)

Weapons of Choice/weaponsofchoice.com (A major national rental house for stage weapons)

APPENDIX C
RECOMMENDED BOOKS

Actors on Guard — by Dale Anthony Girard

The Body Keeps the Score — by Bessel van der Kolk

Combat Mime — by J.D. Martinez

The Illustrated World Encyclopedia of Knives, Swords, Spears & Daggers — Harvey Withers & Tobias Capwell

Fight Choreography — by F. Braun McAsh

Fight Choreography: The Art of Non-Verbal Dialogue — by John Kreng

Fight Directing for the Theatre — by J. Allen Suddeth

Fight Direction — by William Hobbs

Fight Write — by Carla Hoch

Fighting Words — edited by David Blixt

A History of Contemporary Stage Combat — by Brian LeTraunik

Lessons from The Maestro: Crafting a Successful Fight/Stunt Career in Theatre and Film — by David L. Boushey

Manual del Baratero: or the Art of Handling the Navaja, the Knife and the Scissors of the Gypsies — by James Wran

The Medieval Dagger — by Guy Windsor

Movement Directors in Contemporary Theatre — by Ayse Tashkiran
Of Paces — by Payson Burt
The Screen Combat Handbook — by Kevin Inouye
Secrets of the Karambit — by David Seiwert
So You Want To Be A Stuntman — by Robert Chapin
Stage Fighting — by Jonathan Howell
Stage Combat Arts — by Christopher DuVal
Staging Sex — by Chelsea Pace
Staging Trauma — by Miriam Haughton
Stavast; Knife Fighting in the Netherlands — by Jerome Blanes
Swashbuckling — by Richard Lane
The Theatrical Firearms Handbook — by Kevin Inouye
A Terrific Combat!!! — by Tony Wolf

INDEX

Printed in the United States
by Baker & Taylor Publisher Services